Collector's Guide to PEZ

Identification and Price Guide

Shawn Peterson

PEZ

3rd Edition

©2008 Shawn Peterson

Published by

kp krause publications
An Imprint of F+W Publications

700 East State Street • Iola, WI 54990-0001
715-445-2214 • 888-457-2873
www.krausebooks.com

Our toll-free number to place an order or obtain
a free catalog is (800) 258-0929.

PEZ is used throughout this book as a registered trademark. This book is neither endorsed by nor affiliated with PEZ Candy Inc. in any manner

Library of Congress Control Number: 2007934361

ISBN-13: 978-0-89689-635-2
ISBN-10: 0-89689-635-8

Designed by David Jensen
Edited by Karen O'Brien

Printed in Singapore

Contents

Acknowledgments

A very special thank you to:

Maryanne and Paul Kennedy who helped make this book project of mine a reality. When I first got this crazy idea to write a book they allowed me to bring along a photographer and turn their living room into a photo studio back on that fall day in 2000. Thank You! Maryanne is truly one of the most knowledgeable, friendly collectors around and has one of the nicest PEZ collections ever assembled.

My friend Johann Patek who was kind enough to share his time, knowledge, and collection. Johann is one of Europe's leading collectors and has some of the rarest PEZ items known to exist. Not only is Johann an expert PEZ collector, he served as our tour guide, chauffeur, translator, banker, and at one point—the cook! Thanks Johann, it was a trip I will never forget!

Gary Beck and Linda Adams, all I can say is WOW! They have assembled what is quite possibly the finest collection of PEZ dispensers found anywhere in the world. Thank you for your generous hospitality, I enjoyed getting to know you during my visit. Their extensive knowledge and enthusiasm for the hobby is second to none.

Larry Rice for allowing me to visit his home and practice my photography skills. Larry has a wonderful collection of many rare and unusual items. He is a true collector.

Everyone at Pez Candy Inc., for your support and friendship. Mr. Vittoria for taking time out to do the interview for this edition and making Pez fun again!

Nick Petracca candy pack collector extraordinaire. Thanks for your trust and generosity in sending some of those rare packs for me to photograph.

Krause Publications, my project manager Karen O'Brien, Paul Kennedy in acquisitions and everyone who worked on this project, thank you!

My girlfriend Doris who was kind enough to go with me to the PEZ conventions at least once. Thank you for the computer help, support, and understanding during the many, many hours I spent trying to complete this project.

To my #1 sales staff, a.k.a. my parents, John and Lorrene for their continued support and help at ALL of those St. Louis conventions. Thank you!

Thanks to the following people for their help, contributions, and friendship: Silvia Biermayr, Richard Belyski, Mike Chadwick, John Devlin, Gary Doss (The Burlingame Museum of Pez), Dora Dwyer, The Gliha's, Gunter Haidinger, Gerda Jahn (the original Pez lady), Chris Jordan, The Kraft's, Jim Krieb, John LaSpina, Shigeki Ohya (helping with the mini names), my friends at Pez International, Steve Warner (photography 1st and 2nd editions), David Welch for opening the door to this hobby, Jim Williams, and Adam Young.

About the Author

Shawn Peterson started collecting PEZ in 1990 while going to weekend flea markets. At that time he didn't really collect much of anything and just went for something to do. One week he decided to buy a few PEZ dispensers, "I couldn't leave without buying something AND they were just 50 cents apiece." His collection started with about a dozen dispensers, nothing special just common variety footed dispensers, but the collection slowly started to grow. The next year, in 1991, the very first picture book showing all the known dispensers appeared and that was it. "After seeing that book I was hooked, I was on a mission to find PEZ dispensers! I had no idea that there were so many different ones and there was a history to this." What started as a whim quickly grew into an obsession that now takes up much of his free time. "I wouldn't trade it for anything, I've been places and met people from all over the world that I ordinarily wouldn't have, all because of PEZ. PEZ collectors are great. It's really been a lot of fun!"

When he is not roaming the country looking for PEZ or attending a PEZ convention; you can find him at home in the Kansas City area. In addition to PEZ dispensers Shawn also collects KISS memorabilia, vintage candy bar boxes, and "anything else I just can't do without." His collection and books have been the subject of numerous newspaper, magazine, and television stories. Parts of his collection have been on public display at Crown Center and the Toy and Miniature Museum Kansas City as well as featured in *Toy Shop* magazine. He is a contributing writer for the annual *Toys & Prices* books.

Shawn is always interested in adding to his collection or talking to people who used to work for the PEZ Company. You may contact him at:

Shawn Peterson
P.O. Box 571
Blue Springs, MO 64013-0571
pezbook@comcast.net

Foreword

My intent with this book is to offer a reference source that is as complete and informative as possible. I have tried to make this book easy to use, dividing the dispensers into tabbed chapters. For the most part, the chapters, as well as the dispensers, are in alphabetical order to make them easy to locate.

You will also see letters used with various dispensers such as "A," "B," "C," etc. This is used to denote different versions of the same dispenser—"A" being the first or earliest version, "B" the second and so on. The further the letter is in the alphabet the more current the dispenser is.

I hope this book will provide information that both new and experienced collectors will find useful. The best collector is an informed collector, so please take time to study the details and get out and meet your fellow collectors by attending one of many PEZ conventions held each year. With so many things happening in the PEZ world, knowledge is key to a fun and successful hobby.

Please keep in mind, this book is not inclusive of every single dispenser or variation, but should give collectors a broad view of the hobby and dispensers available at time of publication. I have been an avid collector of PEZ for almost 20 years, and I hope you enjoy reading and looking at this book as much as I have enjoyed putting it together.

Shawn Peterson

Invented in 1948, the PEZ dispenser has been around for sixty years. The candy itself has an even longer history dating back some twenty years prior to this event. In 1927, PEZ candy was introduced in Vienna, Austria, as what could possibly be the world's first-ever breath mint. The company marked its 80th anniversary as a brand in 2008.

Edward Haas, an avid non-smoker, wanted to create an item for consumption that would be used as an alternative to smoking. His product—a small compressed sugar tablet with fine peppermint oil—was just the item he was looking for. The mints he created were sold in small pocket-sized tins (similar to the Altoid brand mints of today) and marketed as an alternative to smoking. His slogan was "smoking prohibited—pezzing allowed!" But what is "pezzing," or better yet, PEZ?

The name "PEZ" was derived from the German word for peppermint, "pfefferminz." Using the first, middle, and last letter of the word, Haas came up with the name "PEZ." Nearly twenty years after the candy was created, in 1948, Oscar Uxa invented and patented a little mechanical box for dispensing the candy. Resembling a cigarette lighter, the dispenser offered a hygienic way to share the candy without the risk of having someone else's fingers in your candy tin. This new PEZ "box" invention was quickly marketed as an upscale adult product and had moderate success throughout Europe. In 1952-53 Haas and company decided to expand the product to the American consumer.

In the span of less than two years, it looked as though PEZ was not going to be a viable product for the U.S. market.

Haas did not give up, and the company decided to reinvent the product. They added fruit flavors to the candy and a three-dimensional cartoon head to the top of the dispenser, and marketed the product to children. What a success this turned out to be, combining two of kids' favorite things: candy and a toy! The shift proved to be a brilliant move, making PEZ one of the most recognizable commercial names around today.

It is believed the Full body Santa, Full body Robot, and 1950s space gun were the first dispensers marketed toward children. Due to high production and material cost (and slow sales) this group was discontinued after only a couple of short years. The witch "A" is thought to be the first "traditional" dispenser with a head and stem as we know them today. There has been much debate over the years as to who was the first licensed character to grace the top of a dispenser. However, evidence points to Popeye being the first closely followed by Harvey Comic's Casper the Ghost and Disney's Mickey Mouse.

It is hard to say how many different heads have graced the top of a PEZ dispenser. Different versions of the same character have been produced and, in some cases, the same version has come in multiple color variations. Conservative estimates put the number between 500-600 different heads produced so far.

At any given time there are as many as 20-30 different dispensers available at local retailers, not to mention the seasonal offerings that appear for such holidays as Christmas, Easter, Halloween, and Valentines Day. PEZ began offering limited edition dispensers marketed towards collectors in 1998. Remakes of the classic Psychedelic Hand and Flower were the first to be offered and proved quite popular. Special editions available only through the PEZ Candy Inc., Web site continue to expand and offer collectors more choices and varieties.

PEZ the company is divided into two separate entities, PEZ USA and PEZ International. PEZ USA was located in New York City for the first 20 years of operation. The company expanded and relocated to Orange, Conn., in 1973. Those facilities remained largely unchanged until 2006 when a new warehouse area was added and the front of the building and office area were updated. PEZ USA manufactures the candy, packages the dispensers, distributes and markets the brand throughout North America. PEZ International, now located in Linz, Austria, handles the marketing, manufacturing, and distribution for the rest of the world.

Although they are separately managed companies, they communicate with each other and sometimes work together to produce new dispensers. Functioning as two separate companies explains why some dispensers commonly found in the United States are not found anywhere else in the world, and vise versa.

PEZ Candy Inc. is a privately owned business and does not release sales figures to the public. They acknowledge, however, that more candy packs are sold per year than there are kids in the United States. Their staff works in three shifts, 24 hours a day, producing the candy and packaging dispensers to try and keep up with the ever increasing demand.

The dispenser itself has seen a few modest changes over the years. One of the biggest happened in the late 1980s when "feet" where added to the bottom of the dispenser base to give it more stability when standing upright. Numerous candy and fruit flavors have been produced over the years. Some flavors were more popular than others, and some were just plain strange like chlorophyll, flower, and eucalyptus.

Although PEZ has a long history, it hasn't always been a hot collectible. PEZ collecting has been gathering steam since the early 1990s when the first guidebook appeared depicting all known dispensers and listing their rarity. The first ever PEZ convention was held in Mentor, Ohio, on Saturday, June 15, 1991. Several other conventions around the country soon followed, and collectors finally had the chance to meet each other, buy and sell PEZ, and view rare and unusual dispensers on display. Conventions have quickly become must-attend events for addicted collectors, drawing people from all over the United States, Canada, Europe, and Japan—making PEZ truly an international phenomenon.

In 1993, the prestigious Christie's auction house in New York took notice of this evolving hobby and held its first ever pop culture auction featuring PEZ. The auction realized record prices, taking the hobby to a new level. PEZ has been featured in countless magazines, television shows, and news articles—landing on the cover of Forbes magazine in December of 1993. The popular Seinfeld television show even had an episode featuring a Tweety Bird PEZ dispenser. All of this notoriety has benefited the hobby. More and more people have begun to collect these cute character pieces, sending prices into the hundreds and even thousands of dollars for a single dispenser.

PEZ has done very little in the way of advertising, relying on impulse purchases and parents buying for their kids on a nostalgic whim. While this may not seem like the best marketing method, the company claims it can barely keep up with demand. PEZ is a very popular licensee, with companies vying to put the PEZ name on everything from clocks to coffee mugs.

No one can say for sure where this hobby will go, or if the dispensers will continue to hold their value. In the nearly twenty years that I have been a collector, prices, as well as the collector base, have grown steadily. At present, the hobby has two things in its favor; current demand is surpassing the supply of vintage dispensers, and the fact that PEZ is still produced today makes it available to a whole new generation of potential collectors. Today you can find PEZ in almost any grocery store, discount store, or chain retailer. With new dispensers added regularly, the continued popularity and success of PEZ is almost certainly assured.

Over time there have been a few key dates that really stand out:
• 1949—the first dispenser or "PEZ Box" was patented and produced.
• 1952-53—PEZ makes its debut in America, followed closely by the addition of character heads to the dispenser.
• 1987—some thirty-five years after the first character head was introduced, first real noticeable change happened when feet were added to the dispenser base. Now, almost twenty years later, we are seeing one of the largest changes ever made by the company. The long-standing rule of not putting a real person atop a PEZ dispenser has been broken. This could arguably be THE most significant change to date, and I think 2006 will be regarded as one of the most important years in PEZ history. The possibilities are as varied as are the people who could be included.

In the fall of 2006, the company released a gift set featuring the Teutuls of Orange County Choppers, a real life motorcycle building family featured on a popular cable television show. July of 2007 saw the release of a special, three-dispenser limited edition Elvis Presley gift set. The release of these sets brought a whole new awareness to PEZ and broadened the fan base for this iconic candy.

The addition of real people to its dispensers wasn't the only transformation at PEZ Inc. In late 2004, a new President was named to oversee the U.S. operation and ushered in a number of changes. Communication with collectors increased dramatically, and one of the most visible changes for consumers has been the number and variety of new characters released and sold at retail. PEZ has become very timely, licensing the hottest characters and co-ordinating dispenser production with movie release dates—something unheard of just a few years ago. Perhaps the day may not be far away when tours of the PEZ factory may be offered or even a retail store selling PEZ products may be open to the public.

PEZ marked its 80th anniversary as a candy brand in 2007. It was also the year PEZ introduced a new mini mint marketed to adult consumers. The new container gives a nod to the look of the original PEZ box. Instead of dispensing one mint at a time, the consumer tips the container to dispense. It seems that the product, as well as the marketing, have come full circle. The new design features selected artwork from famous artists such as Norman Rockwell and Andy Worhol. This is another example of PEZ expanding traditional boundaries and introducing the brand to a whole new market.

I feel like I say the same thing every year, "this is the most exciting time to collect PEZ." Every year, however, PEZ seems to top itself and come up with something a little more exciting or different than what has been done in previous years, and these next few years will be no exception. There are some exciting projects in the works and many new characters on the way. I hope as you look through this guide and enjoy the new additions it will create that spark of passion to collect and enjoy each and every dispenser.

For now, sit back, relax and enjoy nearly eighty years of candy dispensing memories!

The original rabbit logo (Haas means rabbit in German).

This is where the PEZ HAAS sign used to hang.

These are the actual letters that used to hang from the building in Vienna. They are now located in California and can be seen at the Burlingame Museum of PEZ. If you look close at the bottom left there is a picture of the letters when they were still attached to the building..

These are the original property markers used to mark the four corners of the factory grounds in Austria. If you look closely at the photo you can see they are carved "Ed Haas 1863."

Interview

Mr. Joseph Vittoria is the President and Chief Executive Officer of PEZ Candy Inc. I was able to meet with Mr. Vittoria on April 11, 2007. Our conversation included putting real people on a dispenser, the PEZ motorcycle, visits to the factory, and what it takes to sell more than 40 million dispensers a year.

Shawn: What is your title and how long have you been with the company?

Joe: President, Chief Executive Officer, and executive board member of PEZ Global.

Shawn: How long have you been with the company?

Joe: Two and one half years.

Shawn: Tell me about your background. What brought you to PEZ?

Joe: Brand consciousness, I guess you could call it. I've always been interested in great brands. I've operated several companies over the years, some of which were leaders in their industry; where the brands were the keynote to how they do business. At one point I had an interest in acquiring PEZ because of its broad brand awareness and strength. The family and/or investors were not interested in selling PEZ. However, several years later I was approached and asked if I would be interested in joining PEZ and head up operating the company. My background before included managing branded consumer products and companies like J. A. Henckels Cutlery, Appliance Corp. of America (Betty Crocker, Welbilt, and Haier Brands) or as a Partner in professional services companies such as Price Waterhouse, Coopers Consulting, IBM Business Consulting, and working with global branded companies in reorganizing their businesses.

Shawn: You said you have been here for 2-1/2 years, in that short time you have made some pretty significant changes with the company. Will you talk a little about some of the things you have done so far?

Joe: The significant changes you've seen, or we've talked about at PEZ include some major changes in the factory operations, several in brand enhancement and development, but generally it's been based on the idea of, 'How do we make more fun out of the business?' Most of the changes we've made are those changes that have to do with how the product represents and what that means to the consumer. Our goal is to bring back or reinforce what is special about PEZ. Those goals are to include being true to keeping the product something special, something that you always remember.

We've introduced products again that capture what I believe is happening in America at a point in time. For instance Orange County Choppers is one of those unique items. Star Wars clearly has captured American's interest. We made the Star Wars collector's set because George Lucas created something that became a key turning point in cinematic history in the United States, and PEZ was perceived as there to celebrate that time. Orange County Choppers is a phenomenon today that brings choppers back into the American psyche. America in the 1960s was enamored with choppers and it represented America at a time of significant change. I am sure you remember Easy Rider. Several other series have come along since American Choppers burst onto the scene. Elvis is another one of those characters that will always be part of American pop culture, just as PEZ is. We've created an Elvis collector set. More importantly, we've tried to make sure that PEZ is no longer seen as a discount store-only item. You now find PEZ in stores for prices for one dispenser ranging from $0.97-$0.99 at Wal-Mart, up to as much as $1.99 for the same item, and collector sets for as much as $19.99 in stores or on eBay at many times that depending on the set.

Shawn: You mentioned Orange County Choppers, in 2006, the long-standing policy of not having a real person on a dispenser was broken. What lead to that decision and why start with the Teutuls?

Joe: There is a movement in the States that is nostalgic, and choppers themselves bring back some of that nostalgia. The Teutuls just happen to be an interesting phenomenon in the United States, and they are great guys. They seem to be bringing the right message. If you know the Teutuls, you know they are against underage drinking and alcohol and drug abuse and pornography in film [and] magazines. They walk the talk and have proven that in the choices they have made in their lives. They are very proud of conquering their addiction and are not afraid to talk about it and I feel they send the right message. That combined with their appeal to the general public is important for us. One of the things we were searching for is something to broaden our audience and re-ignite the young boys and tweens, because we were known for a quite long time as a very young child's product, as well as more for young girls. I think we are changing the perception of PEZ to the U.S. consumer.

Shawn: You worked with Orange County Choppers to have a PEZ themed motorcycle built. How did that decision come about and what are the plans for the motorcycle?

Joe: Call it just a search for fun. We were looking for something that would be exciting, something

that would bring us into the public's eye, or into that 'young male tween' arena and interest. The motorcycle is one of those things that I've been around much of my life and captured my interest when I was young. The Teutuls have created such terrific appeal in the market, that from my perspective it was a natural that we chose to build a chopper. It was something I remember from the '60s and '50s. So when you think about nostalgia and PEZ, this was a great way to marry the two while creating fun and excitement with our brand. I thought this would kick us into high gear as opposed to being the sleeping brand we were. I believe it worked.

The concept for the motorcycle came together after talking to the Teutuls and to Nubb, who's the painter. I said to them, here are the things I want to have relative to themes on the bike. The original PEZ lady, I wanted to include some of the old PEZ standards but definitely wanted to make sure that we also recognized another important event that's happened to America, and that was 9/11. So the bike has got some 9/11 reminders to it. And since we were known for PEZ policeman and fireman, we made the spokes to resemble policemen and firemen dispensers. We had the paint with all themed PEZ items and many of the dispensers we made over time. We have a little Mickey dispenser image carefully painted on it, which Disney was concerned about because of motorcycles. I think we respected Disney's wishes and tradition while at the same time adding a little twist on to the bike. We wanted to make sure we incorporated PEZ nostalgia. We painted the tank in the shape and design of a 1950s PEZ pack. You'll notice it has the original Austrian writing. All the graphics are the original graphics. In fact, Nub used a 1959 or 1960 PEZ pack of candy. So we had the dispenser in the original vendor box that we had found and we had given it to Nub and he had copied it exactly.

Shawn: Even one side of the tank is upside down just as the candy pack is.

Joe: Absolutely!

Shawn: As the president of a company with such a loyal and dedicated fan base, what kind of feedback do you receive from collectors?

Joe: Well it varies, and it's all positive. Some are emotional, some are just excited. I can tell you that so far I've have had a lot of terrific compliments about where PEZ is going. It's the kids, the loyalty of the collector that speaks to what PEZ is and what it's supposed to be. I think that's really the most important message. I get a lot of collectors who want to talk about re-igniting old characters or changing the nostalgic themes, and I think we're doing some of those things as well. It's all been positive. Sometimes we have to maintain some control, the excitement of some collectors, to illegally copy, rebuild, redesign our products and sell them to the market. Trading sites like eBay are a big factor, along with other Internet sites where PEZ is traded. Many things make it to market that demonstrate the excitement of the PEZ collector, some which are not quite 'legal', or infringe on ours or other registered copyrights. However, we can appreciate the flattery while we work to make sure that the PEZ brand is always respected.

Shawn: In the overall big picture of PEZ as a business and by your estimation, how big of a role do collectors play?

Joe: I think that one of the things that makes PEZ successful is the fact that retailers know that it is a collectible product. Do they buy it with the expectation the collector will buy all of them? No, not at all, however, they do realize that there's something PEZ has done to wake up a need or an interest. And that interest is clear. It's a loud message to many retailers and they do understand it. They're hoping they are developing a collector base of their own with the fact that you can get into PEZ, go into their store and buy a PEZ character.

Shawn: How often do you get requests from people wanting to visit the factory and take a tour?

Joe: About 10 to, 20 a day. It depends on the day.

Shawn: Do you see a time when PEZ will allow visitors? Maybe not to the production side of the factory but perhaps a museum and gift shop people can visit and buy all things PEZ?

Joe: Well hopefully both at the same time. One of the things I've been considering for the last two and a half years since I've been here, is how to build a shop that pays homage to PEZ fans; which could be solved by adding a bit of a museum feel with a view to maybe the factory floor so they can see how PEZ are packaged and where they come from.

Shawn: Do you think PEZ will ever take a more active roll in the collector conventions by having a representative regularly attend the various shows and talk to collectors, maybe sell product there?

Joe: We have had people attend, including myself, I've gone into conventions quietly. But one of the things, I think that keeps PEZ somewhat of an unknown, is the fact that we don't actively try and drive the collector community, it happens on its own. When you try too

hard as a company to drive collector groups it seems fake, it doesn't have that real and genuine feel of excitement. So I think that we'll always have an influence in what products are collectible, but I don't think we'll play an active roll in trying to drive or control collectors. That should be something I think the collectors do purely because it's a great product that they love to collect and trade.

Shawn: At this particular point, Spring of 2007, you've shared the your ideas for the Elvis dispenser and that is the next big thing that's going to come out. Is there anything else on the horizon that might be of interest to collectors that you can talk about?

Joe: Oh there's a few items, but not too many. We're trying to limit how much we introduce at one time. We do that because we also don't want to saturate the market nor do we try and make everything collectible. Many companies have tried to do that and learned that you lose the collector's and consumer's interest. We've got Elvis this year and we are really paying homage in some respects to another icon in American pop culture by focusing on Elvis. We're also doing it with a little twist in that we're adding not only a collectible, numerical sequence to it, but we're also adding a 3-song CD specifically produced for the PEZ Elvis set, which are associated with the periods that Elvis was popular much like the three dispensers that are, based on different periods in Elvis' life. This year we are also coming out with a Disney Princesses collector's set, which is similar to the Star Wars box and design, but with an 8-character set. Two of the characters this year will only be available in the set.

Shawn: Do you have any fun facts about the factory, like how many pieces of candy they make or how many dispensers are made or anything like that?

Joe: I can give you some numbers that come out pretty regularly. In the case of tablets, we produce somewhere around 10-12 million tablets a day.

Shawn: A day??

Joe: Yes. Up to a million rolls are produced in a day. We sell in excess of 40 million dispensers in a year. And that doesn't even count some of the other items, like sets or for instance plush. We probably sell over 2 million plush dispensers like Barnyard Babies, Cuddle Cubs and things like that. At this rate, the plush business seems to be growing with key chains and back pack clips and they're becoming very popular, so I'd say the day of 100 million dispensers is not that far away.

Shawn: Generally speaking, can you describe the

day to day operation of PEZ Candy, Inc? What does it take to keep the factory running, such as number of people, how many shifts, amount of raw material used?

Joe: Depending on the time of year we run three shifts, all equipment to no less than three shifts / one equipment. We will on occasion go down to two shifts but it doesn't look like that's happened. We have up to 250 people at times in our factory in operations here in the United States. We keep expanding both with equipment and company size. We just added a fifty thousand square foot extension roughly, which includes a warehouse that is about forty-seven feet tall. It's an interesting place that keeps changing and growing. We've fully rebuilt the facility and offices, and are working on a small collection of our own. We're trying to collect all the PEZ from the past. We are looking to the collector community to get some dispensers because we don't have some of the items that PEZ collectors have.

Shawn: I'm sure when word gets out you'll have letters and offers of people wanting to donate dispensers. What are some of your goals with PEZ? As a brand, where do you see the company in ten years?

Joe: In ten years, well in five years the company will have doubled in its current size. Most of it will be within PEZ. Within the next 2-3 years, we'll probably have doubled the PEZ business alone. We're also looking at acquiring other brands that are very similar—similar in design and nostalgic appeal—brands that the U.S. consumer sees as important. We want to try and create another PEZ because we think PEZ has all the right features of what a brand should have.

"I think we are changing the perception of PEZ to the U.S. consumer."

CHAPTER 2

Pricing Information

A price guide should be viewed as just that—a guide. My goal with this book is not to label a dispenser as being worth exactly "X" amount of dollars but rather a guide to give you a range of what a dispenser may sell for and a reference to help determine what is truly rare. For example, why is one Pony valued at $60 and another color valued at $600? Colors and other slight variations can make huge difference when determining the value or rarity of a dispenser. Since this hobby has become organized, PEZ prices have been in nearly constant motion. Prices not only go up, but in some cases DO go down. Several factors account for this fluctuation: supply vs. demand, emotion, and quantity finds. To pick a point in time and label a dispenser worth exactly "X" amount of dollars, in my opinion, is not in the best interest of the collector or the hobby. I feel that an average price system is more useful. I have used several sources—online auctions, conventions, dealer's listings, and other collectors—to determine what I feel is an accurate price range for each dispenser. Therefore, a price quoted will not reflect the top or bottom dollar that a dispenser has sold for. Dispensers that do not appear for sale often enough to determine an accurate price range will be represented with a price and the "+" symbol.

This pricing information should be used for dispensers that are complete and void of any missing pieces, cracks, chips, or melt marks, and have working spring mechanisms. Dispensers that are broken or missing pieces are not worth nearly as much as complete dispensers. Pricing incomplete or broken dispensers is very subjective. Missing pieces are almost never found. Some collectors don't mind if a dispenser is broken or missing a piece or two, especially if it is a rare dispenser or variation. They may be happy just to have an example in their collection, and hope to upgrade to a dispenser in better condition.

Generally, the value of a dispenser is in the head. Age, country of origin, stem, and patent numbers can also play a part, but are commonly thought of as non-determining factors when assessing the value. Exceptions to this regarding the stems are features such as die-cuts, advertising, or pictures, such as the one found on the Witch Regular. One or more of these features can actually increase the value of the dispenser. Other stem characteristics must be present in certain dispensers to complete the value and be considered correct. For example, the Football Player stem will have one smooth side with an upside down pennant-shaped triangle molded in. Also, all of the original Psychedelics will have at least one, and sometimes two, smooth sides to which a sticker was applied (stickers must still be intact). Swirled or marbleized stems can also add value to a dispenser. Some collectors are willing to pay more for these as they can be very difficult to find and no two are exactly alike. Finally, resale is something you may want to consider. A complete, mint-condition dispenser will always be easier to sell than one that has problems or is missing parts.

Please keep in mind that this book is not inclusive of every single known dispenser variation. This book is meant to be used strictly as a *guide,* the publisher, author or anyone involved with this book are not responsible for any possible loss incurred while selling or buying PEZ dispensers because of information contained in this guide. Use your own best judgment to decide what is best for you when buying and selling PEZ.

A Word of Caution

Collectors beware: Some people have been making and selling reproduction parts for PEZ and more recently fake or reproduction vintage dispensers. Trust your instinct. If you think an item is questionable, it is better to pass than find out later that you have been taken. Know what you are buying and be familiar with what a piece should look like. Remakes and fakes are not limited to just parts, whole dispensers have recently surfaced that are fakes. Some of the vintage dispenser remakes include, but are not limited to; One Eye Monsters, Indian Chiefs, and 1950s Space Guns.

Some dispensers such as KISS or the Beatles for example, were never made by PEZ but can be found with relative ease. How can this be? When a dispenser of a certain character or person is in demand but does not exist, collectors have sometimes resorted to making their own dispensers. These are known as "fan-made" or "fantasy" pieces. Again, some of these pieces are better made than others; in fact some are quite good. You can even find fantasy pieces that are mint on a very convincing PEZ card or even in a sealed poly bag, but in reality were never made by PEZ.

Only knowledge, experience, and buying from a well known, reputable dealer will help avoid having a reproduction or fake unknowingly passed on to you. Common reproduction parts include but are not limited to: the Ringmaster's moustache, the Mexican's goatee and earrings, the Policeman's and Fireman's hat badges, the Knight's plume, the Doctor's reflector, and Batman's cape. Most parts are not labeled as reproductions. For instance, a remake of the doctor's reflector may be made of aluminum instead of plastic, and the reproduction capes for Batman are usually much thicker than the vintage capes. The quality of reproduc-

tion parts has certainly improved. Studying pictures in books and going to PEZ conventions are your best sources for comparing dispensers.

A great deal of information can also be found on the Internet. There are many PEZ related Web sites made by collectors that will answer almost any question related to the hobby. One of the sites I often recommend is the "Pez-Head" group on Yahoo. This site has a wealth of information and a large base of knowledgeable collectors willing to answer questions and share information. The site is located at: http://groups.yahoo.com/group/PEZheads/

How to Use this Guide

The dispensers listed in the first portion of the book are divided into subject categories. The common name of the dispenser is listed first, followed by any alternate names. Next you will find a date—this is the approximate time the dispenser was sold at retail. Notes on whether the dispenser was made with or without feet (or both) are also included.

Finally, a value will be given for the dispenser as well as for known variations.

Values given are for loose dispensers complete with all working parts, and have no melt marks, cracks, or chips. Pricing packaged dispensers is a bit more subjective. Some collectors have little or no interest in packaged dispensers, as they want to display their collections more creatively. Currently, there is little interest in poly bag packaging. Clear cello bags may add some value to a dispenser. For example, if the dispenser is worth $50, it might bring $60-$70 if packaged in a clear cello bag. The exceptions to this are dispensers that are packaged with an insert, sticker, comic, advertising, or a rare pack of candy. Sometimes the inserts or candies are worth more than the dispenser! Dispensers mounted on cards with artwork are considered the most desirable of packaged dispensers. Factors affecting the value of a carded dispenser are condition of the card, graphics, or artwork. Seasonal cards with neat artwork are worth more than plain, solid color cards.

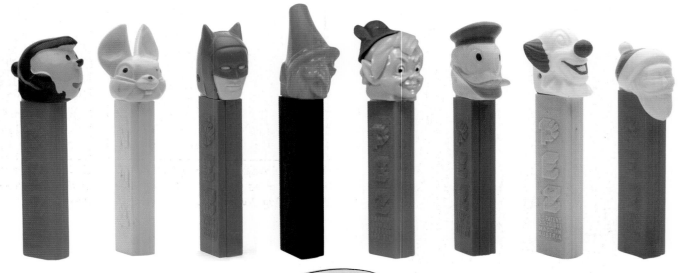

Barky Brown

2005, With Feet

Can be found on 5 different stem colors—the 2006 version can be found with 5 different color crystal heads. These were created by PEZ for Australia's Animal Welfare League as a fund-raiser to help needy animals. 10,000 of each set were produced.

Value: **$15-$25 each**

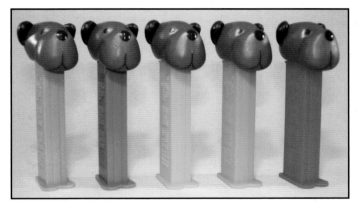

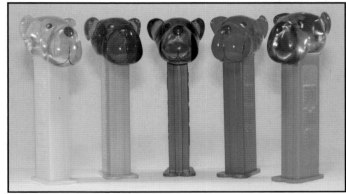

Barky Brown

2005, With Feet

This pair was created by the AWL (Animal Welfare League) of Sydney, Australia, in 2005 to help animals of hurricane Katrina. 2,000 pair were created, and proceeds supported "Paws of the Storm."

Value: **$20-$25 each**

Barky Brown

2006, With Feet

Stenciled stem versions created for fundraiser August 26, 2006.

Value: **$20-$25 each**

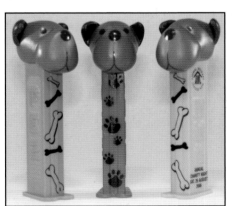

The Animal Welfare League of Sydney, Australia hosted a charity fund-raiser Saturday Aug. 26th 2006.

Cool stenciled stems on the Barky Brown dispensers.

Bugz

Summer 2000, With Feet

The PEZ Web site calls them Barney Beetle, Jumpin' Jack the grasshopper, Florence Flutterfly, Sam Snuffle the fly, Super Bee, Sweet Ladybird the lady bug, the Clumsy Worm, and Good Natured Centipede.

Value: $1-$2 each
Crystal Bugz: $4-$6 each

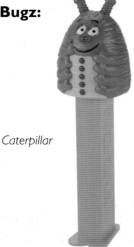

Caterpillar

The "Smart Bee" or Baby Bee.

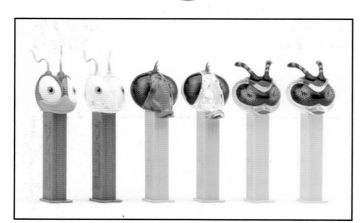

Crystal Bugz; Flutterfly, Fly, and Bee.

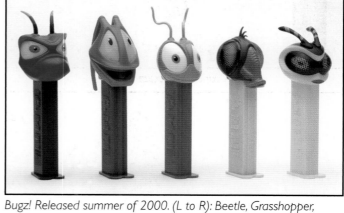

Bugz! Released summer of 2000. (L to R): Beetle, Grasshopper, Flutterfly, Fly, and Bee.

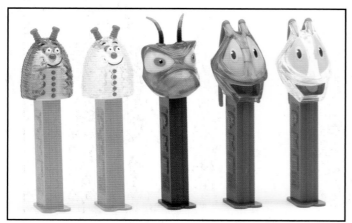

Crystal Bugz; Caterpillar, Beetle, Grasshopper.

Lady bug (Sweet Ladybird as referenced by PEZ International), Crystal Lady Bug, Clumsy Worm, and Crystal Clumsy Worm.

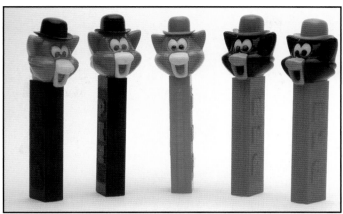

Cat with Derby (also known as Puzzy Cat)

Early 1970s, No Feet

Several head and hat color combinations are available, as are many stem colors. The blue hat version is the rarest, selling for twice that of other versions.

Value: $85-$95
Blue hat: $150-$175

Cat with Derby (or Puzzy Cat). The blue hat version in the center is the rarest and sells for twice that of other versions.

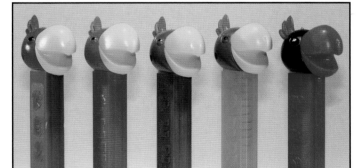

Cockatoo

Mid-1970s, No Feet and With Feet

Several head and beak color combinations are available. The peach-colored beak is harder to find and worth more than other colors.

No Feet: $65-$85
With Feet: $50-$70

A variety of Cockatoos.

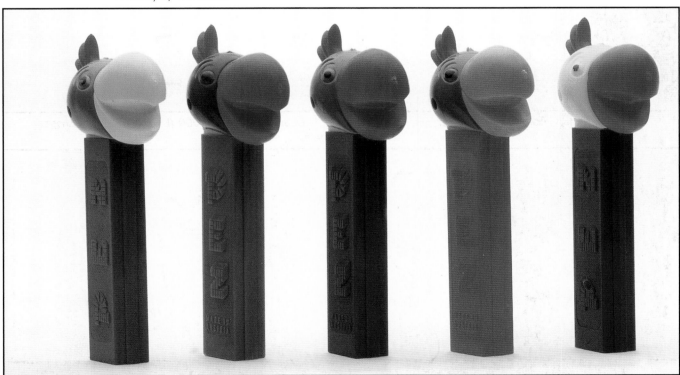

Several color variations of the Cockatoo dispenser. The peach beak version (second from right) is much harder to find.

ANIMALS

Cow A

Early 1970s, No Feet

There are many different color variations of the head. The green and purple heads are rare variations and sell for four to five times as much as other versions.

Value: **$100-$125**

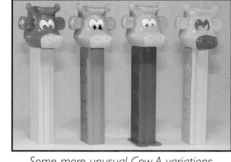

Cow A. The green-head version on the far left is a rare variation.

Some Cow A variations, the two on the far right are extremely rare.

Rare brown Cow A variation.

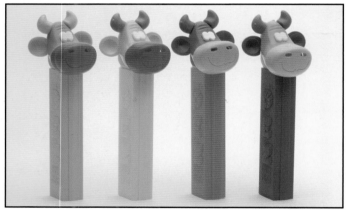

Some more unusual Cow A variations.

Cow B

Mid-1970s, No Feet

Many different color combinations can be found. The same mold was used to make the head for the Yappy Dog.

Value: **$85-$120**

Many color combinations can be found of the Cow B dispenser.

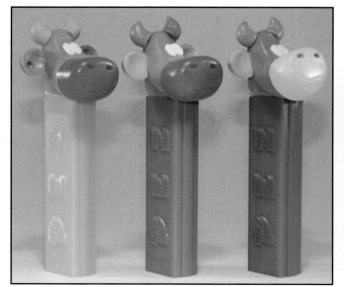

Some Cow B variations.

More Cow B variations.

Crazy Animals

Released Fall 1999, With Feet
Not sold in the U.S.
Four Animals: Frog, Shark, Octopus, and Camel.

Value: **$1-$3**

Crazy Animals (L to R): Frog, Shark, Octopus, and Camel.

Crystal Crazy Animals

Released 2005, With Feet
These odd crystal variations were found in "laydown bags" that contained 30 refills and a single dispenser.

Value: **$4-$8 ea.**

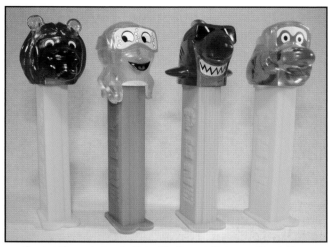

Crystal Crazy Animals (L to R): Camel, Octopus, Shark, Frog.

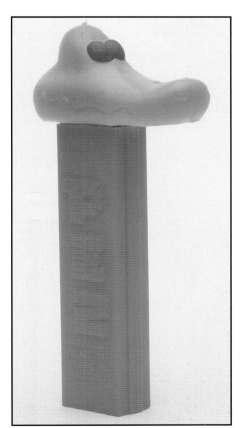

Crocodile from the mid-1970s.

Crocodile

Mid-1970s, No Feet
Can be found in several shades of green and even in purple. The purple version sells for three to four times as much as the green head dispensers.

Value (green head crocodiles): **$100-$125**

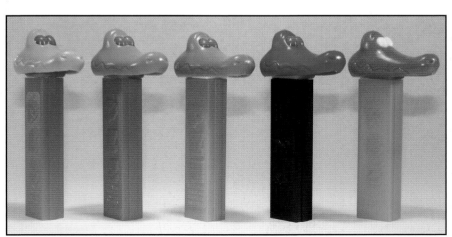

All five color variations known for Crocodiles.

Crystal Dinosaur

1999, With Feet
Only available through a PEZ mail-in offer.
Value: $3-$5

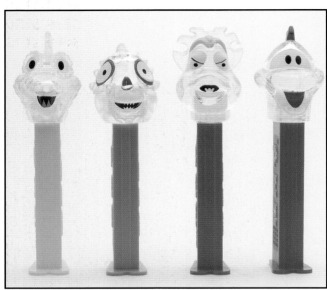

Crystal Dinosaurs. This series was only available through a PEZ mail-in offer.

Duck with Flower

Early 1970s, No Feet
Many head, flower, and beak color combinations can be found. Black, Orange, and Yellow are the hardest head colors to find and usually sell for two to three times as much as other color variations.

Value:	**$85-$125**
Yellow Head:	**$250-$300**
Black or Orange Head:	**$300-$350**

Duck with Flower. Many color combinations can be found of this dispenser.

Dinosaurs

Early 1990s, With Feet
The Dinosaurs were first released in Europe in the early 1990s and were known as the "Trias Family"—Brutus, Titus, Chaos, and Venesia. Shortly thereafter, they were introduced to the United States as "Pez-a-Saurs."
Value: $1-$2

Dinosaurs (L to R): She-Saur, Fly-Saur, He-Saur, and I-Saur.

Some unusual Duck with Flower combinations.

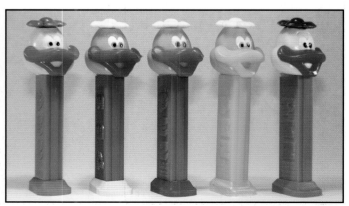

More variations of the Duck with Flower.

Elephant (also known as Circus Elephant or Big Top Elephant)

Early 1970s, No Feet

There are three different variations to the elephant regarding its head gear—flat hat, pointy hat, and hair. The elephant came in many different color combinations, some of which, such as the pink head variation, are tough to find.

Flat hat:	**$100-$125**
Pointy hat:	**$125-$150**
Hair:	**$150-$175**

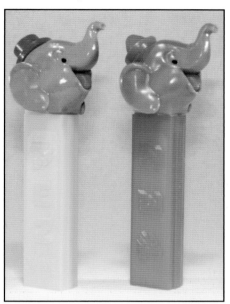

Hard to find gray head Elephant versions.

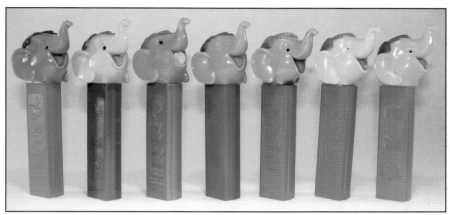

Lots of Elephant variations!

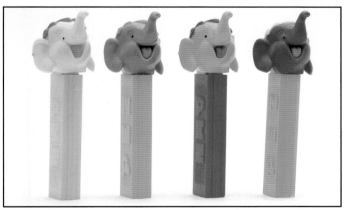

Some variations of Elephant with Hair.

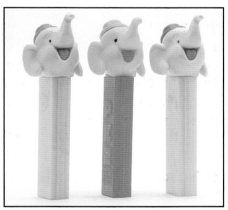

Some variations of Elephant with Flat Hat.

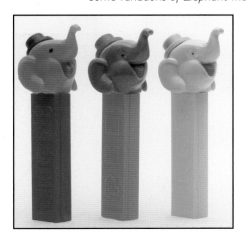

Elephant with Flat Hat.

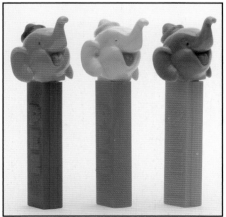

Elephant with Pointy Hat.

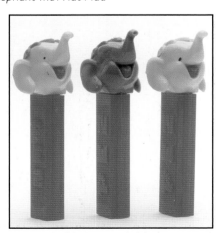

Elephant with Hair.

Elephant—Maximare Elephant

2004 clear / 2005 blue crystal, With Feet

Maximare Bad Hamm is a European water park.

Value: **$10-$15 each**

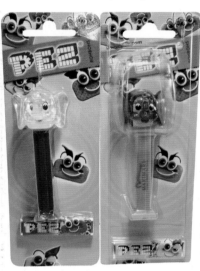

Maximare Bad Hamm is a European water park.

Giraffe

Mid-1970s, No Feet

This is one of the tougher animal dispensers to find.

Value: **$175-$200**

Giraffe from the mid-1970s.

Gorilla

Mid-1970s, No Feet

This dispenser was produced with a black, brown, or orange head.

Value: **$80-$95**

Two examples of the Gorilla.

Hippo

Early 1970s, No Feet

Among the rarest of the animal dispensers, the hippo was not released in the United States and is very difficult to find. The Hippo is unusual in that it has an entire body on top of the stem rather than just a head.

Value: **$900-$1000**

K-9 Crystal Head

2007, With Feet

Produced as a fundraiser item and not sold at retail.

Value: **$100-$125 set of 5**

Crystal K-9 dispensers, special dispensers created in limited numbers, not sold at retail.

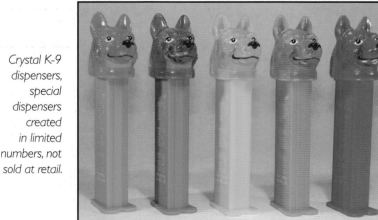

The Hippo was not released in the U.S. and is very difficult to find.

Right side of the Hippo dispenser.

Unique inscription on the stem of the Hippo dispenser.

Kooky Zoo Series

Late 1990s, With Feet

Series includes Blinky Bill, a koala and licensed Australian comic character, Lion, Gator, Hippo, and Elephant. A crystal series of the Lion, Gator, Hippo and Elephant was available in 1999 through a PEZ mail-in offer.

A hot pink Elephant and a tan face Lion were also released by PEZ Candy Inc. as part of their "Misfits" mail-in offer.

Value:	**$2-$6 each**
Crystal Series:	**$3-$5 each**
"Misfit" Elephant	
and Lion:	**$5-$10 each**
Zinnafant Elephant:	**$25-$30**

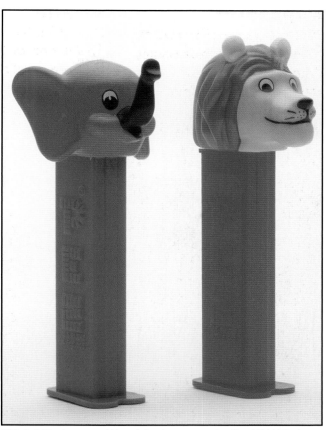

"Misfit" Elephant and Lion (also known as the David W. Lion) were only available through a mail-in offer.

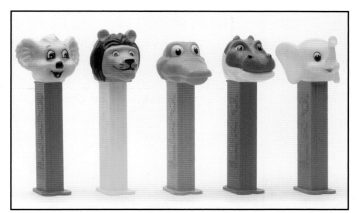

Kooky Zoo Characters (L to R): Blinky Bill (licensed Australian comic character), Lion, Gator, Hippo, and Elephant.

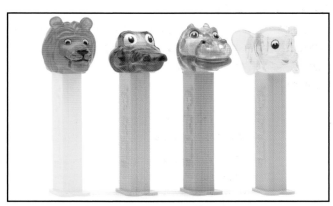

Colored Crystal Kooky Zoo Characters.

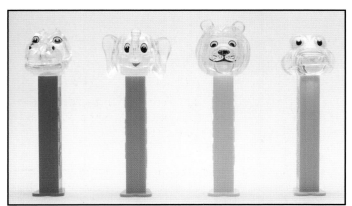

Crystal Kooky Zoo Series (L to R): Hippo, Elephant, Lion, and Gator. This series was only available through a PEZ mail-in offer.

"Zinnafant" Elephant. Done by a European drug company to promote a new antibiotic drug called "Zinnat." Should come with matching candy pack to be considered complete.

Lil Lion

Late 1960s, No Feet
Value: **$70-$90**

The friendly looking Lil Lion from the late 1960s.

Lion with Crown

Mid-1970s, No Feet

This dispenser can be found with several subtle green face color variations and many other different color combinations. The very tough to find red face with white crown goes for twice the price of other variations. Some other rare variations can sell for more than double the price.

Value:	**$125-$175**
Red Face/White Crown:	**$200-$250**

Variations of the Lion with Crown. The very tough to find red face with white crown goes for twice the price of other variations.

Some unusual color variations of the Lion with Crown, the two on the far left are especially hard to find.

Hard to find Lion with Crown variations.

Novartis Lion

2004, With Feet

Promotional item for Novartis pharmaceutical company, the makers of a blood pressure medication in Europe.

Value: $15-$20

The bright red Novartis Lion was a promotional item for a blood pressure medication in Europe.

Lions Club

1962, No Feet

A unique, interesting, and hard to find dispenser. Consul Haas was the president of the Lions Club, Austria. He commissioned the dispensers for the purpose of handing them out to members who attended the 1962 International Lions Club convention in Nice, France. After the convention, the few pieces of remaining stock had the inscribed stem removed and replaced with a generic PEZ stem. It was sold in the Circus assortment.

Inscribed stem: $3000+
Generic stem: $2000+

A red head variation of the Lion's Club dispenser with generic stem.

Lion's Club dispenser with PEZ side of stem showing.

Lion's Club dispenser with Lion's Club inscription.

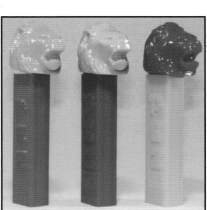

Rare variations of the Lion's Club dispenser.

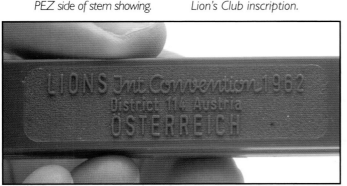

Stem inscription reads: Lions Int. Convention 1962, District 114 Austria, Osterreich.

The red inscribed stem is extremely rare and very difficult to find.

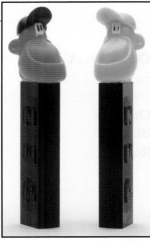

Mimic the Monkey (Also known as Monkey with Ball Cap)

Mid-1970s, No Feet and With Feet

Many different head colors were produced, making this an especially fun dispenser to try and collect all variations.

Mimic the Monkey is also known as "Monkey with Ball Cap."

No Feet:	**$75-$85**
With Feet:	**$65-$75**

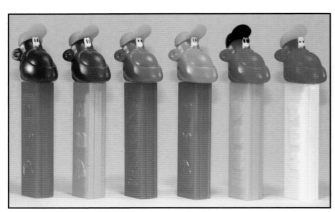

More variations of the Monkey with Ball Cap a.k.a. Mimic the Monkey.

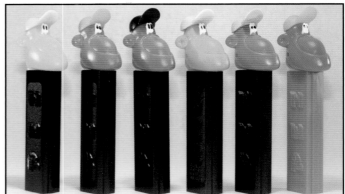

A selection of Mimic the Monkey dispensers. The green variation on the far right is very rare and difficult to find.

Monkey Sailor

Late 1960s, No Feet

The same dispenser was used as Donkey Kong Jr. with one exception, a small transparent sticker was added on his cap with the letter "J." The Donkey Kong Jr. was a 1984 Ralston Purina cereal premium.

Monkey Sailor:	**$60-$80**
Donkey Kong Jr. with box:	**$400-$500**

Monkey Sailor from the late 1960s. The same dispenser, with a "J" added to the cap, was used as a Donkey Kong Jr. dispenser in the 1980s.

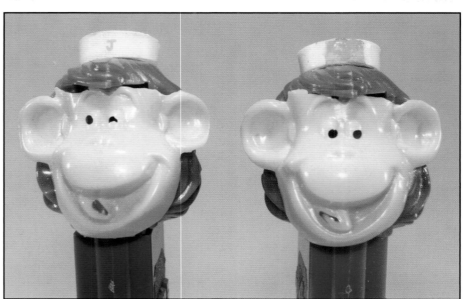

Close up showing the "J" sticker variations of Donkey Kong Jr.

Octopus

Early 1970s, No Feet

The Octopus can be found in red, orange, or black.

Orange:	**$85-$95**
Black:	**$90-$120**
Red:	**$125-$150**

Color variations of the Octopus dispenser.

Two examples of the Octopus.

Rare crystal blue head variation and marbleized stem version on the right.

Panda

Early 1970s, No Feet and With Feet

The Panda has undergone a few modest changes but can still be found today. Rare and hard to find colors include the yellow and red head versions.

Removable eyes version (oldest):	**$25-$35**
Yellow or Red head (with removable eyes):	**$500+**
No Feet, stencil eyes:	**$10-$20**
Current version:	**$1-$2**

Panda (L to R): newest version, Stencil Eyes-No Feet, and Removable eyes.

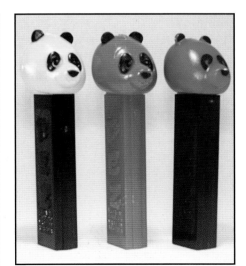

Rare variations of the Panda dispenser.

Two rare variations of the panda—the yellow and red heads.

Panther
Late 1970s, No Feet
Value: $125-$150

Extremely rare Panther variation; few are known to exist with this color combination.

A blue variation of the Pony-Go-Round dispenser.

 *(right column photo of blue Pony-Go-Round dispenser)*

Panther from the late 1970s.

Pony (also known as Pony-Go-Round)
Early 1970s, No Feet
This dispenser can be found in MANY different colors and it's fun to search for variations. Some are very difficult to find such as the green, pink, and purple heads and these versions can bring up to five times as much as the more common color combinations.

Value (common color combinations):   **$100-$150**

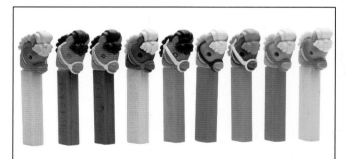

The Pony, also known as the Pony-Go-Round, can be found in many different colors. The green, pink, and purple heads are hard to find variations and can bring up to five times as much as more common color variations.

A selection of Pony-Go-Round variations, the pink head versions are especially difficult to find.

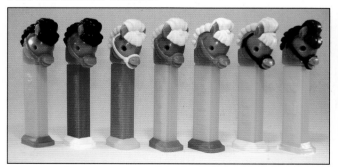

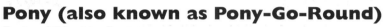 *(brown and green pony variations photos)*

Brown variations of the Pony-Go-Round.

More Pony variations, the green head versions can be difficult to find.

 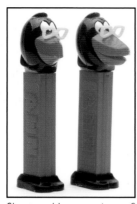

Short and long versions of the yellow-beak Raven. The long beaks are difficult to find.

Short and long versions of the red-beak Raven.

Raven

Early 1970s, No Feet and With Feet
Two versions were made of the Raven—one with a short beak and one with a long beak. The beak can be found in either yellow or red. The long beak was not released in the U.S. and usually sells for about three to four times that of the regular version.

Short Beak, No Feet:	**$75-$90**
Short Beak, Feet:	**$50-$75**
Long Beak:	**$250-$300**

Rooster

Mid-1970s, No Feet
There are several different color variations with white being the most common followed by yellow and green.

White:	**$40-$50**
Yellow or Green:	**$65-$85**

Side-view comparison of the short and long-beak versions of the Raven.

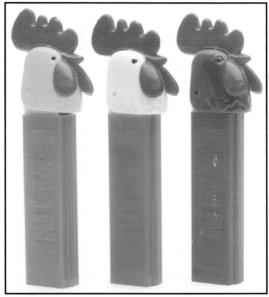

Several color variations can be found of the Rooster—white is the most common, followed by yellow, then green.

Yappy Dog

Mid-1970s, No Feet and With Feet
This head was also used to make Cow B.

Orange head:	**$60-$75**
Green head:	**$70-$85**
With Feet:	**$50-$65**

 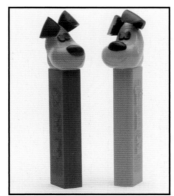 

Two head variations of the Yappy Dog, the version on the right was also used for Cow B.

Yappy Dog—this same head was also used on Cow B.

A selection of Yappy Dog variations, the blue version is extremely rare.

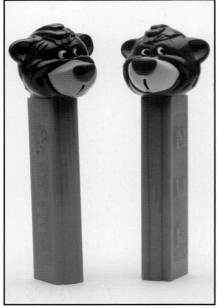

Baloo from the Jungle Book series released late 1960s.

Baloo

Late 1960s, No Feet and With Feet
Although difficult to find, Baloo was also produced with a yellow or red head.

Blue-gray head, No Feet:	**$30-$40**
Blue-gray head, With Feet:	**$20-$30**
Red or Yellow head, No Feet:	**$500+**

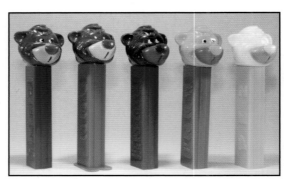

A selection of Baloo dispensers from Disney's Jungle Book, the two variations on the far right are especially rare.

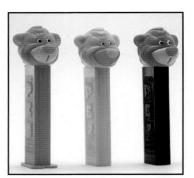

Rare and unusual Baloo variations.

Bambi

Late 1970s, No Feet and With Feet
The same mold was used for the Rudolf dispenser but with a black nose. A rare version of this dispenser, although subtle, carries the copyright symbol along with the letters "WDP" on the head that can at least double the value.

No Copyright, No Feet:	**$45-$60**
No Copyright, With Feet:	**$35-$45**
With Copyright, No Feet:	**$100-$125**

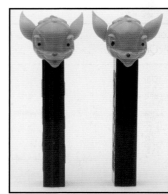

Bambi, from the late 1970s. The same mold was used to make the Rudolph dispenser.

Best of Pixar

2007, With Feet
Mike and Sully from *Monsters Inc.*, Buzz Lightyear from *Toy Story*, and Nemo from *Finding Nemo*.

Value:	**$1-$2**

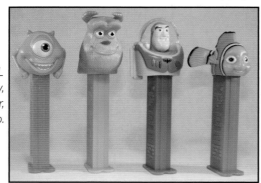

Best of Pixar (L to R): Mike, Sully, Buzz Lightyear, and Nemo.

Captain Hook

Late 1960s, No Feet
A very rare softhead version of this dispenser was produced in the late 1970s, but never went into general production.

Value:	**$100-$125**
Softhead:	**$4000+**

Captain Hook, from the late 1960s.

Cars

2006, With Feet

Early versions of Mater the tow truck (pictured far left) can be found with the entire engine area painted brown. The later and correct version has only the round air cleaner painted. Variations of Doc Hudson and Sally Porsche can be found without the trademark "Hudson Hornet" and "Porsche" on the base of the right side of the car.

Value: **$1-$2**

Cars (L to R): Mater the Tow Truck, Lighting McQueen, Doc Hudson, and Sally Porsche.

Variations can be found of Doc Hudson and Sally Porsche, some have the trademark name "Hudson Hornet" and "Porsche" on the base of the car and some do not.

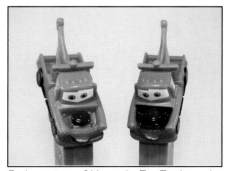

Early versions of Mater the Tow Truck can be found with the entire engine area painted brown (right). The later and correct version has only the round air cleaner painted (left).

Chicken Little

2006, With Feet

Abby, Chicken Little, and Fish Out of Water.

Value: **$1-$2**

Golden Fish Out of Water
(European): **$15-$20**

Chicken Little (L to R): Abby, Chicken Little, and Fish Out of Water.

Chip

Late 1970s, No Feet and With Feet

PEZ only produced one-half of the famous Disney chipmunk duo of Chip and Dale.

Golden Fish Out of Water, a European release.

No Feet:	**$75-$100**
With Feet:	**$50-$75**

Chip, one half of Disney's chipmunk duo of Chip and Dale.

Dalmatian Pup
Late 1970s, No Feet and With Feet
No Feet: $75-$95
With Feet: $60-$75

Daisy Duck
Late 1990s, With Feet
Daisy is a relatively recent addition to the PEZ Disney line-up.
Value: $1-$2

Dalmatian pup, from the late 1970s.

Hard to find variation of the Dalmation Pup.

Daisy Duck, from the late 1990s.

Donald Duck
Early 1960s-Current, No Feet and With Feet

Many versions of Donald have been made over the years. Version D, which has holes in the beak, was also used as the head of the Uncle Scrooge McDuck dispenser. An extremely rare "softhead" version also exists, but never made it to general production.

Version A, (original-early 1960s) sharp, defined feathers, No Feet: $20-$30
Version B, a remake of A with the feathers less defined on top of head, No Feet: $15-$25
Version C, 2 hinge-holes on the side of the head, milky white plastic head, early-mid-1970s, No Feet and With Feet: $15-$25
Version D, 2 hinge-holes on the side of the head, hole in beak, No Feet and With Feet: $10-$20
Version E, produced in the 1980s, came with both light and dark blue eyes: $2-$4
Version F, late 1990s version, the beak is open: $1-$2
Softhead version: $4000+

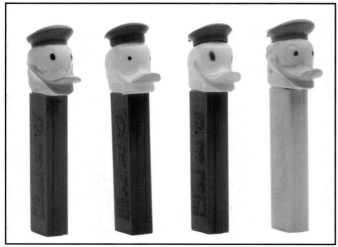

Donald Duck (L to R): Original Version, Version B, (notice the hole in the beak, also used as Scrooge McDuck head), Version C, and remake Version A.

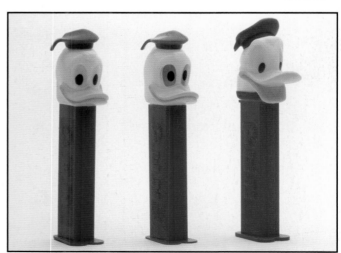

More versions of Donald Duck (L to R): Version E, with light blue eyes, Version E with dark blue eyes, Version F.

Dopey
Late 1960s, No Feet
Value: $150-$200

Dopey from the late 1960s.

Duck Nephews
Originals are from the late 1970s, footed versions are from the late 1980s to 1990s.

Variations can be found of this dispenser with large and small pupils. The early version is also known as "Duck Child" and was only produced with blue or green hats; the later versions were produced with red hats, in addition to blue and green.

Originals: $30-$40
With Feet: $5-$10

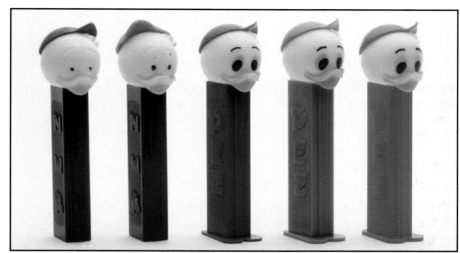

Duck Nephews, originals are from the late 1970s, footed versions are from the late 1980s to 1990s.

Ducktails
Early 1990s, With Feet
Gyro Gearloose: $5-$8
Bouncer Beagle: $5-$8
Webagail or Webby: $5-$8

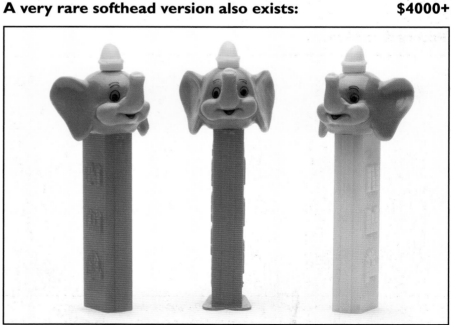

Ducktails, from the early 1990s. (L to R): Gyro Gearloose, Bouncer Beagle, and Webagail or Webby.

Dumbo
Late 1970s, No Feet and With Feet
No Feet: $40-$50
With Feet: $30-$50
A very rare softhead version also exists: $4000+

Dumbo, from the late 1970s.

Extreme Disney

2003, With Feet
Extreme Disney with feet: Mickey, Minnie, Pluto, Goofy, Donald, and Daisy.

Value: $1-$2 each

Extreme Disney (L to R): Mickey, Minnie, Pluto, Goofy, Donald, and Daisy.

Goofy

1970s to current, No Feet and With Feet
Several Goofy dispensers have been produced over the years. Versions A, B, and C can be found with several face color variations.

Goofy, Version B with several face color variations.

Goofy A, removable ears, teeth, and nose, No Feet:	$30-$45
Goofy B, removable ears and teeth, No Feet:	$25-$35
Goofy C, removable ears, No Feet:	$25-$35
Goofy C, With Feet:	$15-$25
Goofy D, late 1980s, green hat, With Feet:	$2-$5
Goofy E, Current:	$1-$2

Goofy, Version C with several face color variations.

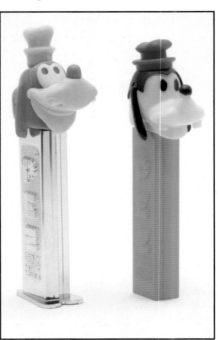

Unusual variations of Goofy.

Goofy, Version D (left) and Version E.

Incredibles
2004, With Feet
Dash, Helen Parr, Bob Parr, and Jack Jack.
With Masks (USA version): $1-$2
No Masks (European version): $3-$5
Golden Jack Jack movie promo: $15-$20

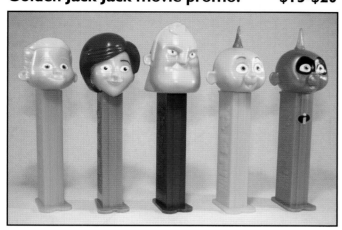

Incredibles (L to R): Dash, Helen Parr, Bob Parr, and Jack Jack (USA versions with mask).

Incredibles (L to R): Dash, Helen Parr, Bob Parr, Jack Jack, and Golden Jack Jack (European versions without mask).

Jiminy Cricket
Early 1970s, No Feet
With many small pieces making up his costume, Jiminy Cricket is a tough dispenser to find complete.
Value: $200-$225

Jungle Book
2003, With Feet
European release. Shere Khan, Bagheera, Mowgli, Baloo, Golden Baloo, and Kaa. Golden Baloo is a European movie promo.
Value: $3-$4 each
Golden Baloo: $10-$15

Jiminy Cricket, from the early 1970s. He is commonly found to be missing pieces, making this dispenser tough to find complete.

Jungle Book (L to R): Shere Khan, Bagheera, Mowgli, Baloo, Golden Baloo, and Kaa. (European release)

King Louie
Late 1960s, No Feet and With Feet

No Feet:	**$30-$45**
With Feet:	**$25-$35**
Rare and unusual	
color variations:	**$500+**

Some unusual and hard to find variations of King Louie.

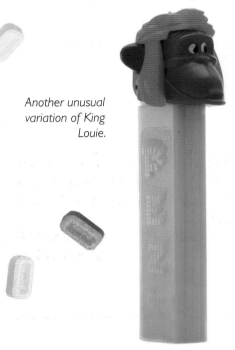

Another unusual variation of King Louie.

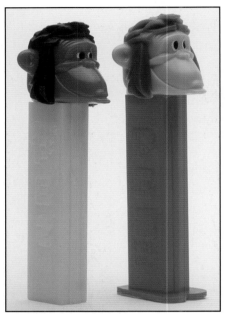

Rare and unusual color variations of King Louie.

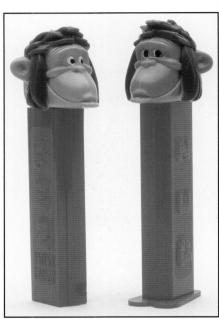

King Louie, from the late 1960s.

Lil Bad Wolf
Mid-1960s, No Feet and With Feet

No Feet:	**$30-$50**
With Feet:	**$20-$35**

Lil Bad Wolf, from the mid-1960s.

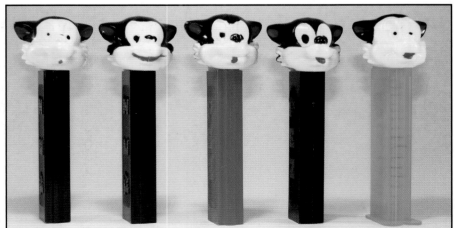

Some variations of Lil Bad Wolf.

Lion King

2004 With Feet
Nala, Timon, Mufasa, Pumbaa, and Simba.
Value: **$1-$2 each**

Lion King (L to R): Nala, Timon, Mufasa, Pumbaa, and Simba.

D
I
S
N
E
Y

Mary Poppins

Early 1970s, No Feet
This dispenser is very difficult to find. As pictured, an even harder to find "painted cheek" variation. One rumor has it this dispenser was in early production when Disney didn't approve the likeness causing PEZ to halt further distribution, and making this a true rarity!
Value: **$850-$1000**
Painted cheeks: **$1000-$1200**

Mary Poppins from the early 1970s. This painted cheek version is extremely rare.

Three different versions of Mary Poppins.

Version on the left has a copyright and version on the right does not.

Meet the Robinsons

2007, With Feet
Carl, Wilbur, Bowler Hat Guy, and Lewis.
Value: **$1-$2**

Meet the Robinsons (L to R): Carl, Wilbur, Bowler Hat Guy, and Lewis.

Mickey Mouse

Early 1960s-Present, No Feet and With Feet

Mickey Mouse has been one of the most popular PEZ dispensers over the years and has gone through many variations.

Die-cut stem with painted face, early 1960s:	**$300-$400**
Die-cut face, early 1960s, No Feet:	**$100-$125**
Version A, removable nose, early 1970s, No Feet:	**$20-$30**
Version B, molded nose, early 1980s, No Feet:	**$15-$25**
Version B, With Feet:	**$10-$15**
Version C, stencil eyes, 1990s:	**$2-$3**
Mickey and Minnie Mouse, current release:	**$1-$2**
Softhead version (rare):	**$4000+**

Rare test mold of Mickey Mouse. (From the Johann Patek collection)

Mickey Mouse with die-cut face, also from the early 1960s.

Mickey Mouse die-cut with painted face, from the early 1960s. This is the rarest of all Mickey Mouse dispensers. (From the Maryann Kennedy collection)

Rare variations of the painted face Mickey Mouse. It is argued that the painted face Mickey Mouse (pictured far left) is the first character head to appear on a dispenser base. This version does not have an applied copyright, and only two are known to exist like this. (From the Johann Patek collection)

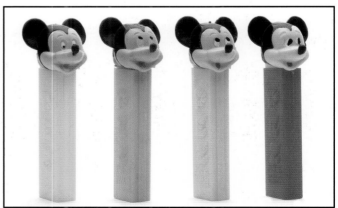

Mickey Mouse variations.

Mickey Mouse with "removable nose" or version A, from the early 1970s. The nose piece was also used as Popeye's pipe!

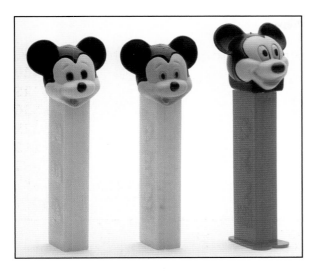

Mickey Mouse B from the early 1980s, and Mickey Mouse C (far right) from the 1990s.

Mickey Mouse D and Minnie Mouse, late 1990s edition.

Mickey Mouse 80th Anniversary

2007, With Feet

This full figure Mickey comes in three different versions; Steam Boat Willie, pie-eyed Mickey and contemporary Mickey. Dispensers are packaged in a clear plastic tube with retro styled peppermint candies. Each package has the special 80th anniversary logo. Net profits from European sales will be donated to charity to help children. A special black and gray version of Mickey and Minnie was also done in 2007 for the Japanese market.

Euro tubes:	**$5-$10**
Japanese 80th anniversary set:	**$30-$40**
Japanese 80th anniversary set w/ crystal heads	**$30-$40**

These were done for the Japanese market to celebrate the 80th anniversary of PEZ in 2007.

Full figure Mickey's standing tall atop the dispenser. (L to R): Steam Boat Willy, pie-eyed version, and a contemporary version round out this trio.

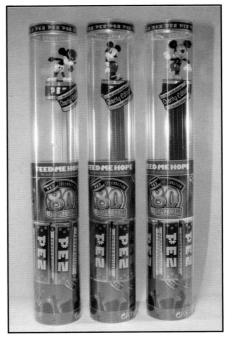

Cool new dispensers and packaging to celebrate PEZ's 80th anniversary!

Mowgli
Late 1960s, No Feet and With Feet

No Feet: $30-$40
With Feet: $25-$35

Mowgli, from the late 1960s.

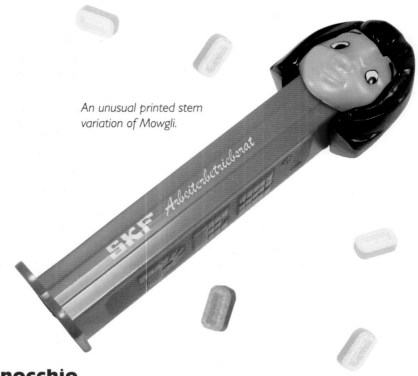

An unusual printed stem variation of Mowgli.

Pinocchio
Early 1960s, No Feet

Two versions of Pinocchio were made—one in the early 1960s and the other in the early 1970s. The earlier version (A) can be found with either a red or yellow hat.

Version A: $175-$225
Version B: $140-$165

Peter Pan
Late 1960s, No Feet
Value: $150-$175

Peter Pan, from the late 1960s.

An unusual blond hair version of Peter Pan.

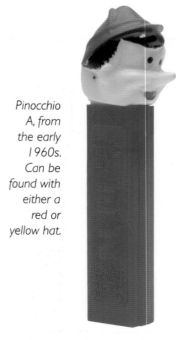

Pinocchio A, from the early 1960s. Can be found with either a red or yellow hat.

Pinocchio B, from the early 1970s.

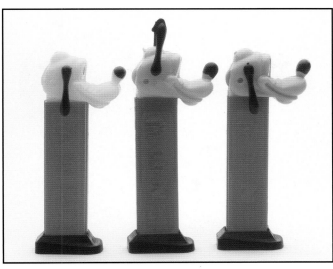

Pluto

Early 1960s-Current, No Feet and With Feet
Several versions of Pluto, Mickey Mouse's faithful dog, have been produced through the years.

Version A, round head and movable ears, No Feet:	**$25-$30**
Version A, "Hong Kong":	**$20-$25**
Version B, flat head and movable ears:	**$10-$15**
Version C, molded ears:	**$2-$5**
Version D, (Current):	**$1-$2**

Pluto, first appeared in the early 1960s. (L to R): Original "Hong Kong" Version, Original Version, and caramel color variation of the original.

A couple of unusual Pluto variations.

Pluto, the two on the left are Version B and are sometimes called the "flat-head version," Version C is second from right, and on the far right Version D.

Practical Pig

1960s, No feet and With Feet
Two versions were produced—the earlier version (A) has a flat hat, and the later version (B) produced in the 1970s, has a wavy hat.

Version A, No Feet:	**$35-$50**
Version A, With Feet:	**$25-$35**
Version B, No Feet:	**$40-$60**
Version B, With Feet:	**$30-$40**

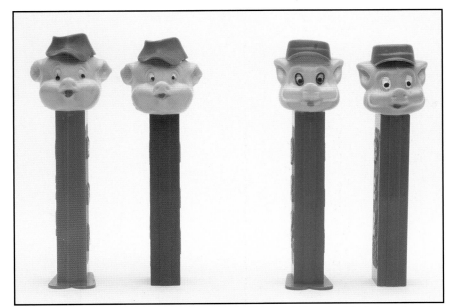

Practical Pig, Version B from the 1970s is on the left; Version A from the 1960s is on the right.

Princesses

2005-Present, With Feet
2005: Princess Jasmine from *Aladdin*, Belle from *Beauty and the Beast*, and Cinderella. 2006: Aurora from *Sleeping Beauty* and Ariel from *The Little Mermaid*. 2007: Snow White. 2007: A gift set was issued with all the princesses and two new additions—Mulan and Pocahontas.
Value: **$1-$2 ea.**

Disney Princesses (L to R): Princess Jasmine from Aladdin, *Belle from* Beauty and the Beast, *Cinderella, Aurora from* Sleeping Beauty, *Ariel from* The Little Mermaid, *and Snow White.*

Scrooge McDuck

Late 1970s, No Feet and With Feet
The original version used the same mold that was used for Donald Duck Version B, with the glasses, sideburns, and hat as separately molded pieces (and easily lost). The remake version has molded sideburns.

Original, No Feet:	**$30-$40**
Original, With Feet:	**$25-$35**
Remake version:	**$5-$8**

Ratatouille

2007, With Feet
Remy, Emile, Linguini, Skinner.
Value: **$1-$2 ea.**

Ratatouille (L to R): Emile, Linguini, Remy, Skinner.

Scrooge McDuck. Original version on the left is from the late 1970s. Remake version is on the right.

Softheads (Disney)

Late 1970s

These dispensers are ultra rare and were never sold to the public. The few that are known to exist have come from former employees of PEZ. There are six dispensers in this group: Pluto, Donald Duck, Goofy, Captain Hook, Dumbo, and Mickey Mouse.

Value: **$4000+ each**

Disney softheads. Ultra rare and never sold to the public. The few that are known to exist have come from former PEZ employees. Shown here are Goofy, Donald, and Pluto.

Extremely rare Disney Softheads (L to R): Mickey Mouse, Pluto, and Goofy.

Disney Softheads were never produced for the general public and the heads were never put on stems. The stems here are for display purposes.

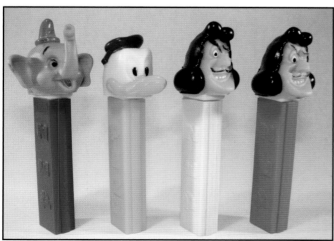

Extremely rare Disney Softheads (L to R): Dumbo, Donald Duck, and Captain Hook.

Disney Softheads, back of head reads, "® Walt Disney Productions Hong Kong."

D
I
S
N
E
Y

Snow White

Late 1960s, No Feet
Collar color variations include white, yellow, turquoise, and blue. Turquoise is worth slightly more.
Value: $200-$225

Thumper

Late 1970s, No Feet and With Feet
A very subtle yet pricey variation of this dispenser has the copyright symbol along with the letters "WDP" on the head.

No Feet, No Copyright: $85-$100
With Feet: $60-$80
With Copyright: $200+

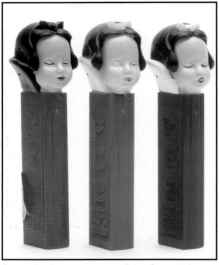

Several color variations of the Snow White dispenser.

A selection of Thumper variations.

Bambi's companion Thumper.

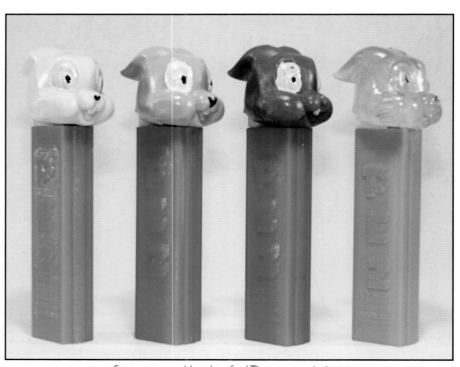

Some rare and hard to find Thumper variations.

Tinkerbell

Late 1960s, No Feet

Value: $200-$250

Tinkerbell, from the late 1960s.

A selection of Tinkerbell variations.

Winnie the Pooh

Late 1970s, No Feet and With Feet

This dispenser was initially released only in Europe. Winnie the Pooh has been quite popular among collectors in general. Remade and re-released in the summer of 2001, Winnie the Pooh and friends can now be found in the U.S.

No Feet:	$75-$100
With Feet:	$65-$85
Remakes:	$1-$3
Roo and Lumpy (2004):	$1-$3

Winnie the Pooh, released in the late 1970s but not in the U.S.

Winnie the Pooh remakes. Released in 2001 and can be found in several minor variations such as the line/no line version of Eeyore (pictured) and gray/no gray paint on the back of the necks of Tigger and Piglet.

Winnie the Pooh (L to R): Roo and Lumpy.

Zorro

1960s, No Feet

This dispenser can be found in several different versions: small and large logo and variations of the hat and mask. Some versions have a curved mask and others have a straight mask.

Versions with logo: $100-$125

Non-logo: $75-$100

Rare black stem version: $2000+

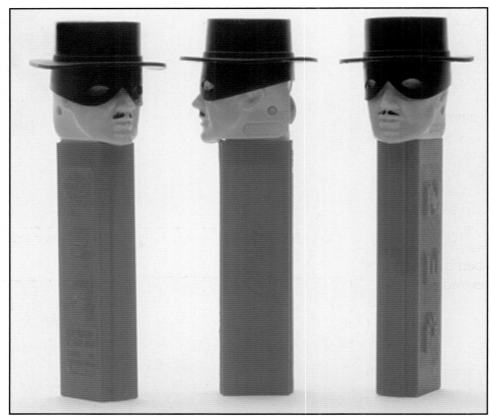

Zorro from the 1960s. The dispenser in the center has the "Zorro" logo stem.

An extremely rare black stem version of Zorro with logo.

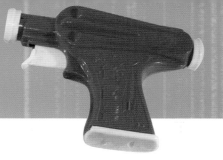

Candy Shooters

Mid-1960s

These dispensers actually shoot PEZ candy! Candy shooters can be found in black and red (as shown) as well as blue, green, and orange. The blue and green guns are very difficult to find and command much higher prices.

In 2006 a large supply of orange candy shooters was found in Europe. Prices came down briefly making these popular during convention bingo games, and some collectors were known to have candy shooting wars during the convention. The additional find seems to have been absorbed by the hobby and prices have leveled off.

Brown:	**$100-$125**
Red or Orange:	**$60-$80**
Blue or Green:	**$350-$500**

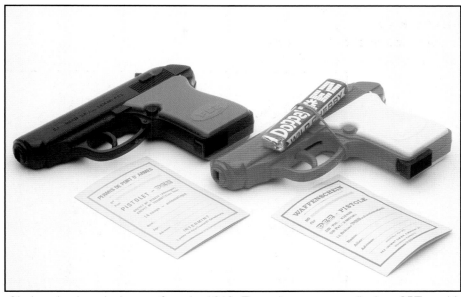

Black and red candy shooters from the 1960s. These dispensers actually shoot PEZ candy!

A Candy Shooter on its original card—very difficult to find.

Backside of the Candy Shooter card with a target for kids to cut out and take aim.

An earlier version of the Candy Shooter card that never had a gun mounted on it.

The half acrylic version on the top was used to test the internal workings during production. The acrylic portion would be fitted to a randomly selected gun by a factory worker and checked to make sure the mechanisms worked properly.

Front and back of candy shooter mint on card.

WOW! European PEZ factory workers with a table full of 1950s space guns!

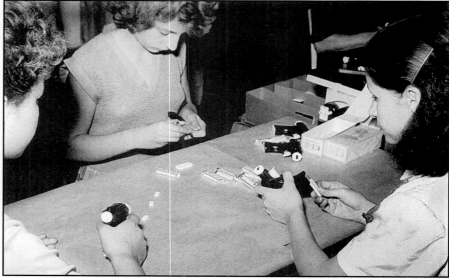

Test firing the space gun. Notice the old candy packs have the "PEZ Box" regular on the back.

Space Guns

1950s

Space guns also shoot PEZ candy and are very desirable among collectors. They were offered as a mail-in premium as well as sold in stores until the early 1960s. They can be found in many different colors. A word of **CAUTION**: In late 2006/early 2007 fakes or reproductions of these guns popped up. The plastic used to make these fakes warps after a short time when tensioned with the rubber band of the trigger. Be very cautious when buying a rare or unusual color. Unless you can actually touch and feel the gun, it is difficult to tell the difference between a reproduction and a legitimate gun.

Red, Yellow, or Green:	**$350-$500**
Black or Blue:	**$400-$500**
Maroon or Silver:	**$850-$950**
Light Blue, Lavender, Gold:	**$3000+**
Transparent (few known to exist):	**$5000+**

Space guns from the 1950s on the original counter display card. Each card originally held six guns. A very rare item, especially in this condition.

A very difficult to find premium offer featuring the 1950s space gun. This 3 panel sheet has the following inscription inside; "A PEZ GUN FREE OF CHARGE- Collect 136 Pez wrappers and stick them onto the squares designed for this purpose. When the folder is filled hand it in to your dealer or send it directly to the address cited on the last side. Your effort will pay. In turn, you will obtain a span-new Pez gun free of charge which to possess you will be envied by all your friends." ("Span-new" is an actual typo) $200+.

An assortment of hard to find and rare '50s gun variations.

An assortment of 1950s space guns.

Three different known blue variations of the space gun.

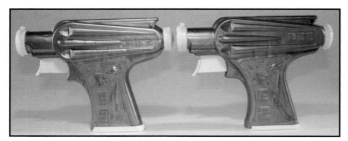

Rare silver and gold variations of the space gun.

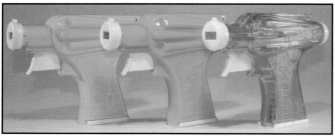

Yellow variations of the '50s gun, the transparent version on the far right is extremely rare.

Extremely rare variations of the '50s space gun.

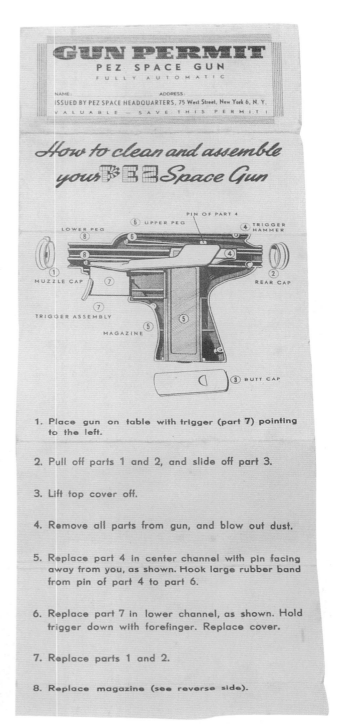

GUN PERMIT

PEZ SPACE GUN

FULLY AUTOMATIC

NAME: _____ ADDRESS: _____

ISSUED BY PEZ Space HEADQUARTERS, 75 West Street, New York 6, N. Y.

VALUABLE — SAVE THIS PERMIT!

How to clean and assemble your PEZ Space Gun

1. Place gun on table with trigger (part 7) pointing to the left.

2. Pull off parts 1 and 2, and slide off part 3.

3. Lift top cover off.

4. Remove all parts from gun, and blow out dust.

5. Replace part 4 in center channel with pin facing away from you, as shown. Hook large rubber band from pin of part 4 to part 6.

6. Replace part 7 in lower channel, as shown. Hold trigger down with forefinger. Replace cover.

7. Replace parts 1 and 2.

8. Replace magazine (see reverse side).

This 1950s space gun permit is valued at $50 to $75.

WOW! A very rare example of a clear 1950s space gun.

An example of a 1950s space gun card. These were used in a retail store to display up to six guns and are extremely difficult to find.

G
U
N
S

49

1980s Space Gun

PEZ produced another space gun in the 1980s to capitalize on the space craze caused by the *Star Wars* movies. Two versions exist, a Hong Kong version and an Austrian version. PEZ later sold the gun molds to a Chinese company who produced the "DSH Space gun." Instead of shooting candy the guns shot plastic pellets in the shape of a piece of PEZ candy. These are very difficult to find.

Silver Space Gun:	**$100-$150**
Red Space Gun:	**$85-$125**
DSH guns:	**$250+**

1980s silver space gun.

1980s red space gun.

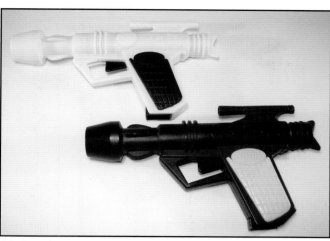

Black and white variations of what used to be the PEZ space gun.

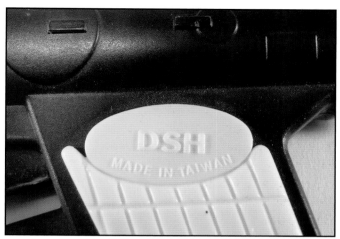

Remake of the PEZ space gun now with the DSH name.

Detail of the "Made in Hong Kong" version.

Detail of the "Made in Austria" version.

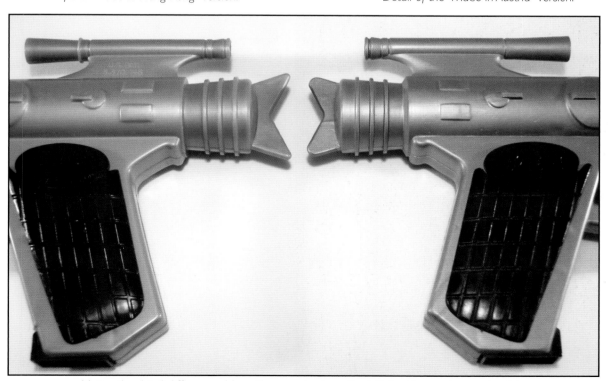

Notice the detail differences, Hong Kong version is on the left, Austrian version on the right.

CHAPTER 6
Holiday

Christmas

Angel

Early 1970s, No Feet and With Feet
Several versions of the angel have been produced, including one with a small plastic loop on the back of her hair that allows it to be used as an ornament.

No Feet:	**$85-$100**
With Feet:	**$50-$65**
Unusual blond hair version:	**$90-$125**
Ornament:	**$100-$125**

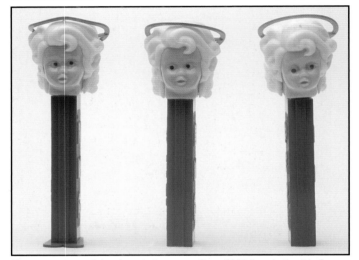

Three versions of the Angel dispenser. (L to R): Yellow hair with feet, yellow hair without feet, and the rare blond version.

Unusual Angel variations, the one on the left is the "loop" version and the one on the right has removable eyes, yellow hair, and a larger than normal halo.

Icee Bear

1990s, With Feet
The earlier version of Icee Bear was not issued in the U.S. The version on the far right made its debut in the 1999 Christmas assortment. It was revised in 2002.

Early Version, left and center:	**$5-$10 ea.**
Far right:	**$1-$3**
Current:	**$1-$2**

Icee Bear. The ones on the left and in the middle were not issued in the U.S. The version on the right debuted in the 1999 Christmas assortment.

Rudolph

Late 1970s, No Feet and With Feet
The mold used to produce Bambi was also used for Rudolph—but the nose on Rudolph was painted red.

No Feet: $50-$75
With Feet: $35-$50

TOTAL CANDY NET WEIGHT 0.56 oz. AVDP or 17 g
Made by HAAS FOOD MFG. CORP., ORANGE, CT 06477 U.S.A.

Rudolph was made from the same mold as the Bambi dispenser—but Rudolph's nose was painted red.

Rudolf on an old, oversize Christmas card.

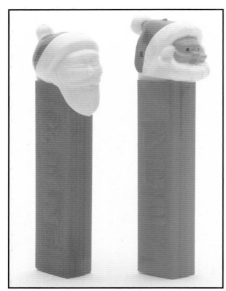

Santa A (left), from the late 1950s; Santa B (right), from the 1960s.

Santa

1950s-Present, No Feet and With Feet

Santa is one of the most popular PEZ dispensers ever produced. Most commonly found is Santa C, which has been produced since the 1970s.

Santa A, No Feet, face and beard are the same color:	**$120-$150**
Santa B, No Feet, flesh-colored face with white beard:	**$125-$160**
Santa C, No Feet:	**$5-$10**
Santa C, With loop for ornament:	**$35-$50**
Santa C, With Feet:	**$2-$3**
Santa D, With Feet:	**$1-$2**
Santa E, (Current):	**$1-$2**
Mrs. Clause With Feet, newest edition to the Christmas series (2006):	**$1-$2 ea.**
Full Body Santa (1950s) made in Austria:	**$150-$200**
Full Body Santa (1950s) made in Germany:	**$250-$350**

Full Body Santa, from the 1950s. This version of St. Nick measures approximately 3-1/2" from boots to hat and is very popular with collectors.

Santa C. This is a VERY common dispenser. (L to R): Version C no feet; Version C with loop on the back of his hat to be used as an ornament; Version C with feet; and Version D.

Full Body Santas in the original counter box! This box is very difficult to find and few are known to exist. Also pictured is an original insert that came rubber-banded around each Santa. The insert had instructions for loading the dispenser and an offer for a Golden Glow. Box: $125-$200; Insert: $20-$30.

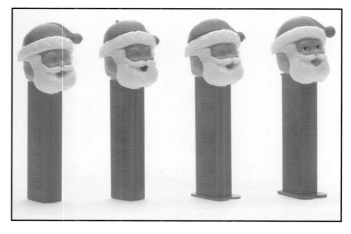

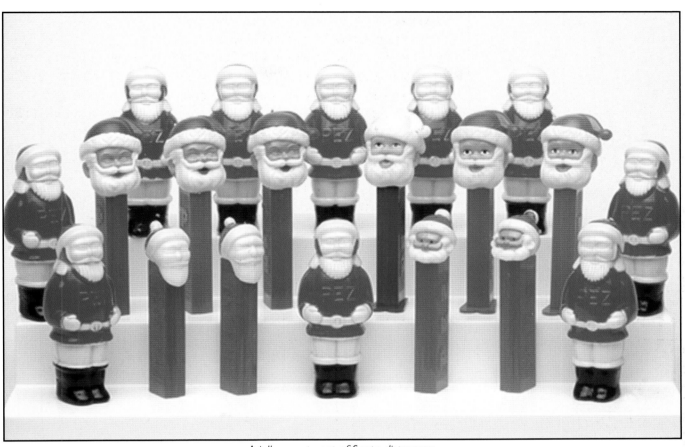

A jolly assortment of Santa dispensers.

Rare variations of the Santa C dispenser. If you look close, you can see the clear Santa has a different "folded" plastic spring instead of the traditional wire spring.

Rare variations of 'ole St. Nick.

Unusual variation of the Santa C dispenser.

Jolly ole Santa's better half: Mrs. Clause.

Full body Santas in an
extremely rare counter box.

Snowman

1970s, No Feet and With Feet

No feet:	**$15-$25**
With feet:	**$1-$5**
"Misfit" versions	
(mail-in offer, late 1990s):	**$5-$8**

The Snowman first appeared in the 1970s. The two dispensers on the far right are "Misfit" versions from the late 1990s.

New Christmas holiday dispensers released Fall of 2002: Santa E, Snowman, Winter Bear, Elf, and Reindeer.

Clear Crystal Christmas

2005, With Feet
Reindeer, Santa, Snowman and Elf and Holiday Bear. Mail order set from Pez.com.

Value: **$4-$6 each**

2005 mail-order offer from the PEZ company.

Easter

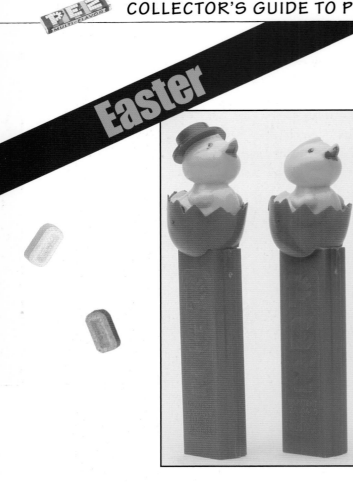

Chick in Egg

Early 1970s-Current, No Feet and With Feet

The earliest versions of this popular dispenser have a brittle plastic eggshell with jagged points. The second version has a thin flexible plastic shell with more uniform points that resemble a saw blade. The third version, from the 1980s, has a much thicker shell but with the same type of points as on the second version. The next version is also a thicker plastic but there are fewer points on the shell and edges are more rounded.

Chick in Egg, No Hat, No Feet:	**$85-$120**
Chick in Egg A, With Hat, No Feet:	**$75-$100**
Chick in Egg B, With Hat, No Feet:	**$15-$25**
Chick in Egg C, With Hat, No Feet:	**$10-$15**
Chick in Egg C, With Hat, With Feet:	**$5-$10**
Chick in Egg D, With Hat, With Feet:	**$2-$3**
Chick in Egg E, With Hat, With Feet (Current):	**$1-$2**

On the left is the Chick in Egg A with hat old version with thin, brittle shell. Notice the steel pin. On the right is the Chick in Egg, no hat, this is the oldest version.

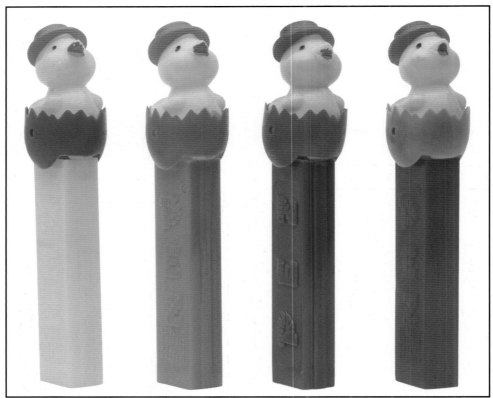

Chick in Egg B with hat, from the 1970s. This second version has a thin flexible plastic shell with more uniform points that resemble a saw blade.

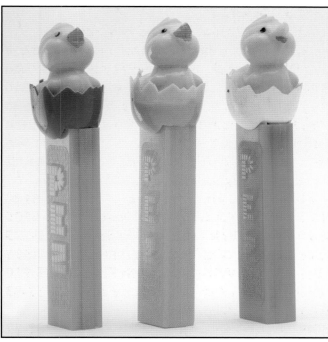

Three variations of the Chick in Egg without hat.

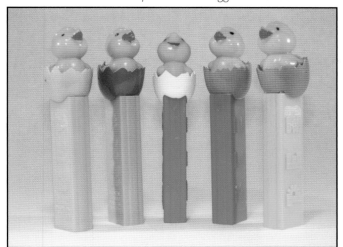

A selection of chick in the egg dispensers without hats.

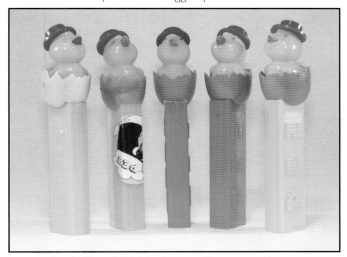

A selection of chick in the egg dispensers with hats.

Chick on Easter card. The graphics make this piece very desirable: $150-$200.

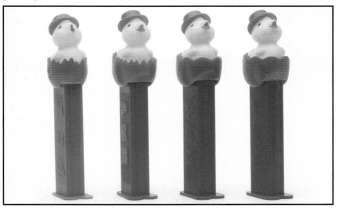

More recent versions of the Chick in Egg with hat from the 1980s to current. The dispenser on the far left is Version B with feet, Version C is next to that, and the two on the right are Version D.

Easter Bunny

1950s-Current, No Feet and With Feet

Bunny A, No Feet, 1950s:	**$200-$250**
Bunny B, No Feet, 1950s:	**$250-$300**
Fat Ear Bunny, No Feet, 1960s-1970s:	**$25-$40**
Fat Ear Bunny, With Feet:	**$10-$20**
Bunny D, 1990s:	**$2-$4**
Bunny D, pink, from the Glew misfit collection:	**$35- $40**
Bunny E:	**$1-$2**

This color variation was created for a certain dealer back in the late 1990s and not sold at retail.

Easter Bunny (L to R): Bunny A from the 1950s; Fat Ear Bunny from the 1960s and 1970s; Bunny D from the 1990s; and Bunny E.

Bunny B from the 1950s. This is a tough one to find.

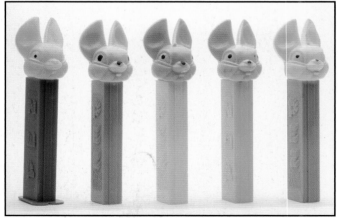

Various Fat Ear Bunnies. These can be found in many different color shade variations.

A selection Fat Ear Bunnies.

Lamb
1970s, No Feet and With Feet

No Feet: **$20-$30**
With Feet: **$1-$3**

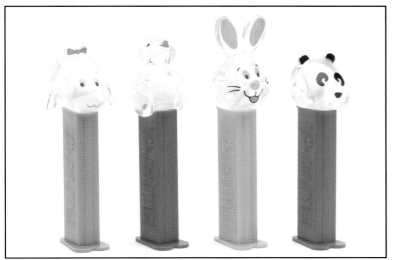

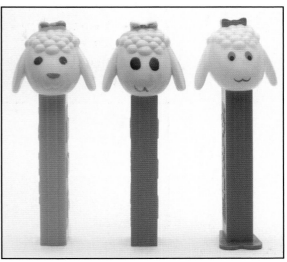

New crystal holiday dispensers—Lamb, Chick, Rabbit, and Panda. Only available through PEZ mail-order offer.

Three versions of the Lamb dispenser.

Carded dispensers such as this are very popular with collectors because of the cool artwork.

Easter (Current)
2004, With Feet
Chick in Egg, Pink Bunny, Baby Face in Egg, and Lamb.

Value: **$1-$2 ea.**

This group was first offered for the 2004 Easter season.

Halloween

Halloween Crystal Series

1999, With Feet

This series was only available through a PEZ mail-in offer. The series includes a Jack-o-Lantern and three different ghosts.

Value: **$3-$5 each**

The Halloween Crystal Series was released in 1999 through a PEZ mail-in offer.

Halloween Ghosts

Late 1990s, With Feet

This non-glowing series was available in the U.S. for only a couple of years. Characters include: Naughty Neil, Slimy Sid, and Polly Pumpkin. These do not glow in the dark.

Value: **$1-$2 each**

Halloween ghosts, the U.S. version from 1999-2001. These do not glow in the dark.

They actually glow in the dark!

Halloween Glowing Ghosts

Late 1990s, With Feet

This glowing version first sold only in Europe, not released in the U.S. assortment until 2002. Characters include: Happy Henry, Naughty Neil, Slimy Sid, and Polly Pumpkin.

Value: **$1-$2 each**

Halloween glowing ghosts. From left to right: Happy Henry, Naughty Neil, Slimy Sid, and Polly Pumpkin.

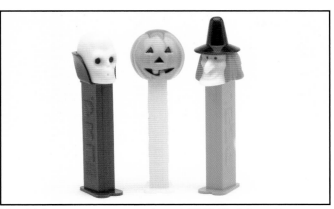

New Halloween assortment released 2002: Skull, Pumpkin, and Witch.

They glow!

Jack-o-Lantern

1980s, No Feet and With Feet

Version A, die-cut face, no feet:	**$20-$25**
Version A, with feet:	**$10-$15**
Version B:	**$2-$3**
Version C:	**$1-$2**
Version D glows in the dark (current):	**$1-$2**

Jack-o-Lantern (L to R): Version A; Version A with feet; Version B; and Version C.

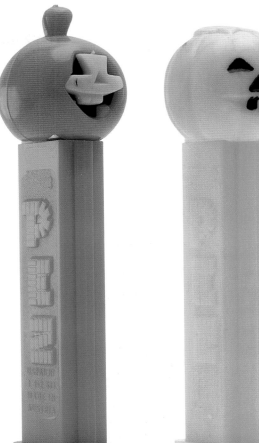

Hard to find two-tone Jack-o-Lantern.

Rare pumpkin variation.

Some pumpkin variations; the one in the middle is extremely rare, the one on the far right is known as the two-tone version and is very difficult to find.

Skull

Early 1970s-Current, No Feet and With Feet
A "misfit" version of the skull with a black head was available in 1998 through a mail-in offer. A very hard to find variation of version B is known as the "Colgate" skull because he has a full set of teeth!

Version A, No Feet:	$15-$20
Version A, With Feet:	$10-$15
Version B, larger head:	$1-$3
Version B, glows in the dark:	$1-$3
"Misfit" version:	$5-$8
Full set of teeth (sometimes called the Colgate Skull):	$50-$60

Skull (L to R): Version A; Version A with feet; Version B with larger head; and "Misfit" Version.

This hard to find skull variation is known as the "Colgate" skull because he has a nice full set of teeth!

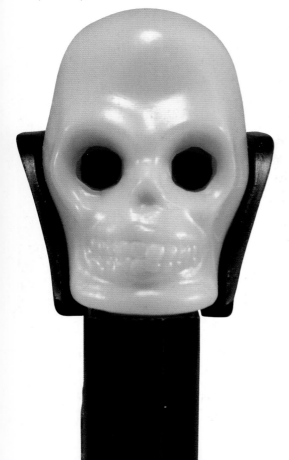

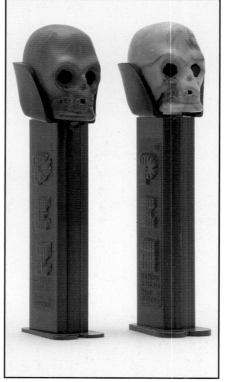

Rare marbelized Skull variations.

Two variations of the Clear Crystal Skull.

Set of old Halloween dispensers on cool old graphic cards.

This set of Halloween first appeared for the 2005 holiday season, the black cat came out one year later in 2006.

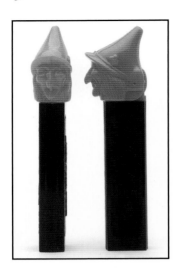

Witch

Late 1950s-Current, No Feet and With Feet

Witch A, orange head, No Feet, 1950s:	**$200-$250**
Witch B, orange head, slightly taller hat than A, No Feet:	**$3000+**
Three-piece Witch, No Feet, 1970s:	**$20-$30**
Three-piece Witch, No Feet, unusual color combinations:	**$100-$150**
Three-piece Witch, With Feet:	**$3-$5**
Witch C:	**$1-$2**
Witch C, glow in the dark version:	**$1-$2**
"Misfit" version (late 1990s):	**$5-$8**
"Convention witch":	**$15-$20**

Witch A from the late 1950s.

The Witch B has a slightly taller hat than version A. The picture on the stem is even slightly different when you compare the two.

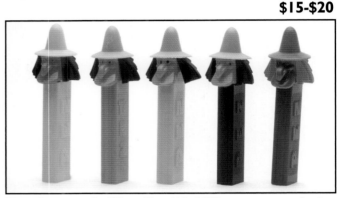

This is known as the "Three-Piece Witch." Shown are unusual color combinations of this dispenser.

More common versions of the Three-Piece Witch from the 1970s.

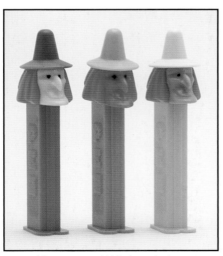

More unusual Witch variations.

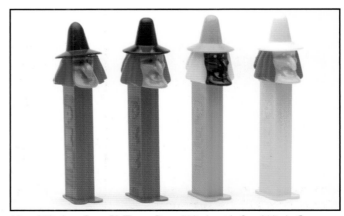

Witch B, this is a very rare dispenser.

More Witches (L to R): Three-Piece Witch with feet; Witch C; two "Misfit" versions.

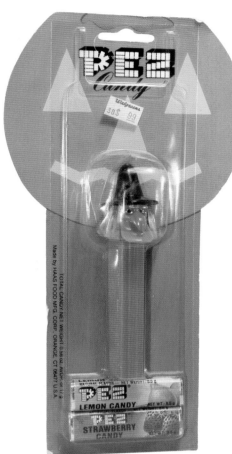

Three-Piece Witch on a die cut pumpkin card, these cards are very difficult to find.

Holiday Crystal Series
1999, With Feet
This series was only available through a PEZ mail-in offer. The series includes Santa, Snowman, Witch, and Skull.

Value: **$3-$5 each**

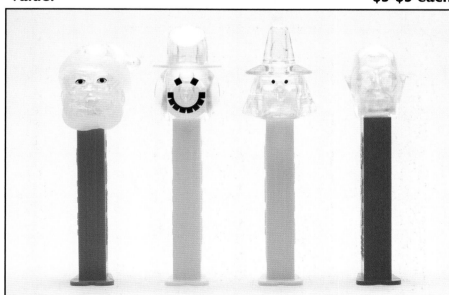

Holiday crystal series. Santa, Snowman, Witch, and Skull dispensers released in 1999 through a PEZ mail-in offer.

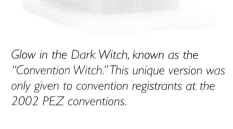

Glow in the Dark Witch, known as the "Convention Witch." This unique version was only given to convention registrants at the 2002 PEZ conventions.

Boy and Girl on Valentine cards from the late 1980s/early 1990s.

Valentine

1970s-current, No Feet and With Feet

Boy and Girl PEZ Pals on die-cut Valentine cards, No Feet, 1970s:	**$150-$200 each**
Boy and Girl PEZ Pals on Valentine cards, With Feet, late 1980s/early 1990s:	**$15-$20 each**
Valentine hearts, red stem, No Feet:	**$1-$3**
Valentines hearts, unusual pink stem, No Feet:	**$125-$150**
Valentine hearts printed stems:	**$1-$2 each**

Newer Valentine hearts on cards.

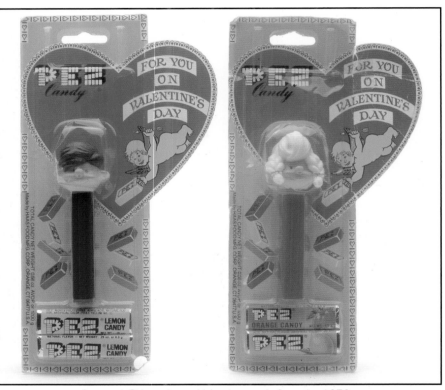

Boy and Girl on die-cut Valentine cards from the 1970s.

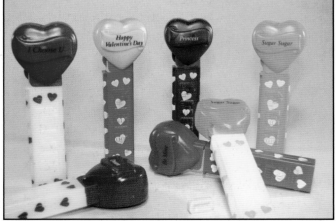

With thirteen different sentiments and many different color combinations the possibilities are almost endless!

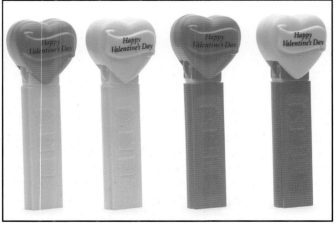

Valentines hearts. The two on the left are a very unusual pink stem variation; the other two are common.

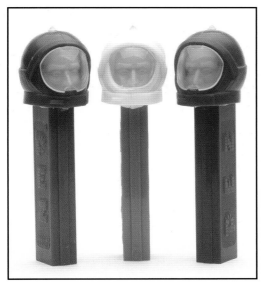

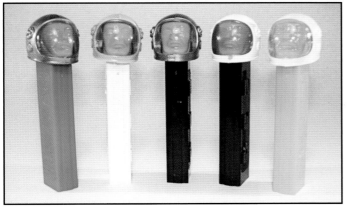

Astronaut B, from the late 1970s.

An assortment of hard to find Astronaut A's.

The stem inscription of the rare "World's Fair Astronaut" from the 1982 World's Fair held in Knoxville, Tennessee. This dispenser is one of two known to exist. Notice the name "Tennesse" is spelled incorrectly—it's missing an "e" on the end. Nobody knows for sure why this one was never distributed. Was it scrapped because of the misspelling, or did it not get approved or licensed for some other reason? Who knows, to date, it's one of those great Pezzy mysteries!

Astronaut A, from the early 1960s. This dispenser was not released in the U.S. and is very difficult to find. It can also be found with a white or light blue helmet.

Astronaut A variation.   *Rare variation of Astronaut B.*

Astronaut

Early 1960s, No Feet

The Astronaut A was not released in the U.S., but the second Astronaut, released in the 1970s was distributed in the U.S. A very rare version of this dispenser exists and is known as the "World's Fair Astronaut" because of the inscription on the left side of the stem. Only two of these dispensers are known to exist—one with a green stem and white helmet and the other with a blue-green stem and matching helmet.

Astronaut A:	**$600-$700**
Astronaut B white helmet/green stem:	**$125-$150**
Astronaut B blue helmet/blue stem:	**$140-$160**
World's Fair Astronaut:	**$5000+**

Betsy Ross
Mid-1970s, No Feet
Value: $125-$150

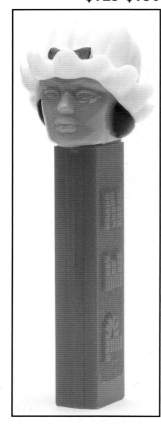

Betsy Ross from the Bicentennial series released in 1975.

Captain (Also known as Paul Revere)
Mid-1970s, No Feet
This dispenser should have a sticker on the left side of his hat to be considered complete.
Value: $150-$175

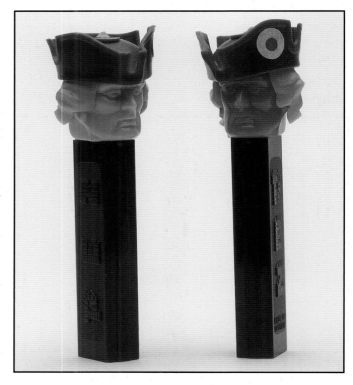

Captain, also known as Paul Revere. He should have the sticker on the left side of his hat as shown to be considered complete.

Cowboy
Early 1970s, No Feet
Value: $250-$300

Cowboy, from the early 1970s.

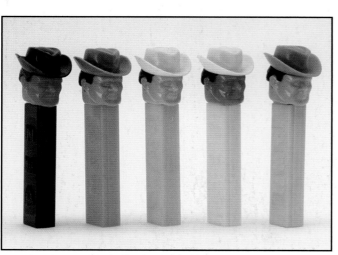

Cowboy variations.

Daniel Boone
Mid-1970s, No Feet
Value: $175-$200

Daniel Boone from the Bicentennial series released in 1975.

Football Player

Mid-1960s, No Feet

This dispenser can be found in either red or blue and will either have a tape strip on the helmet (as shown) or a plastic strip that snaps on the front and back of the helmet. This version is very tough to find. The blank side of the stem with the triangle allowed kids to customize the dispenser with a pennant-shaped sticker of their favorite team.

Tape-strip Helmet:	**$150-$175**
Snap-on Stripe:	**$300-$350**

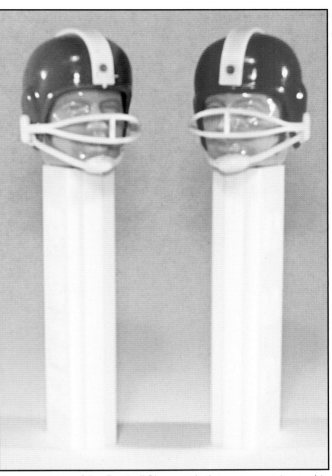

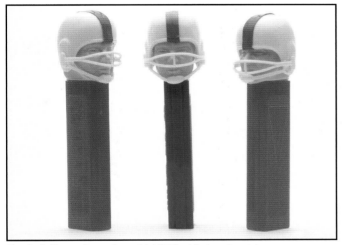

Football Player, from the mid-1960s. Notice the unique stem—the blank side with the triangle allowed kids to customize the dispenser with a pennant-shaped sticker of their favorite team.

Two examples of the Football Player with the snap on stripe on his helmet. This variation is very difficult to find.

Original Football Player counter box from the 1960s.

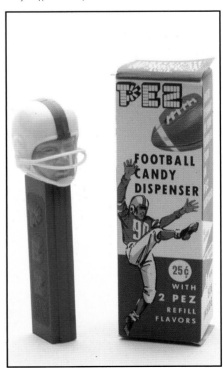

Football Player with original vending box.

Indian Chief

Early-1970s, No Feet

The swirled headdress combinations are virtually endless. It is rumored the plastic used to make the headdress was molded from the ground up and re-melted remains of unsold Make-a-Face dispensers. CAUTION: watch out for reproductions!

Value:	**$125-$150**
White headdress:	**$100-$125**

Indian Chiefs, from the 1970s. The swirled headdress combinations are virtually endless. It is rumored the plastic used to make the headdress was molded from the ground up, re-melted remains of unsold Make-a-Face dispensers.

Indian Maiden

Mid-1970s, No Feet

Value:	**$125-$150**

Indian Brave

Early-1970s, No Feet

Value:	**$100-$150**

The Indian Brave (L) was released in the early 1970s. The Indian Maiden (R) was part of the Bicentennial series released in 1975.

Pilgrim

Mid-1970s, No Feet

The Pilgrim can be found with either a white or yellow hatband.

Value:	**$125-$150**

Pilgrim from the Bicentennial series released in 1975.

Pilot

Mid-1970s, No Feet

Pilot:	**$175-$200**

Stewardess

Mid-1970s, No Feet

Stewardess:	**$175-$200**

Pilot and Stewardess, from the mid-1970s.

Spaceman

Late 1950s, No Feet

A premium version of the Spaceman was offered by Cocoa Marsh in the late 1950s. The premium version had "Cocoa Marsh" on the stem. Several stem variations include light blue, dark blue, and metallic blue, as well as clear or transparent blue helmet.

Value:	**$150-$175**
Cocoa Marsh Spaceman:	**$175-$225**

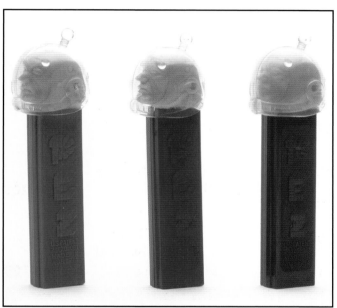

Spaceman dispenser, from the late 1950s. Same as the Cocoa Marsh Spaceman except this one has the PEZ logo on both sides.

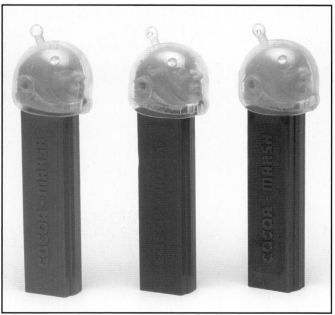

Cocoa Marsh Spaceman dispenser offered as mail-in premium in the 1950s. Cocoa Marsh was chocolate flavored syrup "milk booster."

Uncle Sam

Mid-1970s, No Feet

Value: **$125-$150**

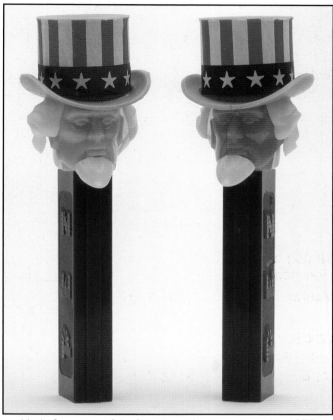

Uncle Sam, part of the Bicentennial series released in 1975.

Wounded Soldier

Mid-1970s, No Feet

Value: **$125-$150**

Wounded Soldier form the Bicentennial series released in 1975.

CHAPTER 8

Japanese

The Japanese mini dispensers made their debut in the spring of 2004. Since then a steady release schedule has offered a new series almost every month in vending machines throughout Japan. Each dispenser is fully functioning and operates just like its full size counter part. Designed to be sold in vending machines, the minis are packaged in a plastic egg that serves as the vending capsule and are sealed with a printed plastic band. Each egg and band are specific to the series, making the packaging an integral part of collecting minis. Each egg comes packed with one dispenser, a small sample pack of candy, and an insert that shows all of the characters in the series.

Because of the bulk and additional shipping weight, many of the minis that have found their way to the United States have been sold as dispensers only, making the collectible packaging tough to find. Produced and marketed by Bandai, the minis are licensed by PEZ. Licensed PEZ items are such a vast category—I haven't covered many of the licensed items in past books. Currently there is a lot of interest among collectors with the minis, so I felt they should be included.

'Gacha' vending machine for the minis.

Hard to find display for the mini cell phone strap holders.

Barbapapa

May 2005, With Feet

A French children's book character. Barbabeau, Barbabright, Barbapapa, Barbamama, Barbazoo.

Loose:	**$15-$20 set**
With Packaging:	**$20-$25 set**
Vending card:	**$5-$10**

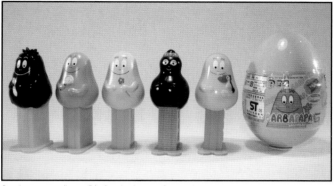

Barbapapa (L to R): Barbabeau, Barbabright, Barbapapa, Barbamama, Barbazoo.

Vending card for the Barbapapa series.

Boukenger

Febuary 2007, With Feet

Boukenger is a Japanese Tokusatsu TV series. Special set sold as retail promotion and not in vending machines. Pictured in box are Bouken Black, Bouken Blue, Bouken Red, Bouken, Pink, and Bouken Yellow.

Value:	**$50-$60 in box**

Capybara-San

April 2007, With Feet

A Capybara is a character used in many of the Japanese claw vending machines. Set includes Namakemono-Kun (Namakemono-Kun means lazy person or idler), Regent-Kun, White San, Capybara-San (with 4 leaf clover) and Capybara-San (normal).

Loose:	**$15-$20 set**
With Packaging:	**$20-$25 set**
Vending card:	**$5-$10**

Vending card for the Capybara-San series.

This Boukenger set was never sold in vending machines, only in the gift box as shown.

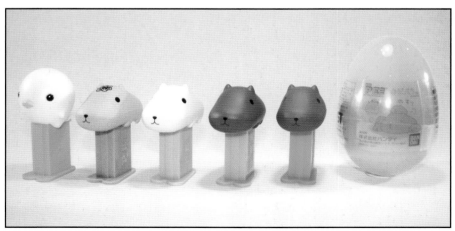

Capybara-San (L to R): Namakemono-Kun, Regent-Kun, White San, Capybara-San (with 4 leaf clover) and Capybara-San (normal).

Dokodemo-Issyo I

September 2004, With Feet

Dokodemo-Issyo are characters for Play Station games. Characters include Toro, Jun, Rickey, Pierre, Suzuki, and Kuro.

Loose:	**$20-$25 set**
With Packaging:	**$25-$30 set**
Vending card:	**$5-$10**

Vending card for the Dokodemo-Issyo series.

Dokodemo-Issyo I (L to R): Toro, Jun, Rickey, Pierre, Suzuki, and Kuro.

Dokodemo- Issyo 2

May 2006, With Feet

Dokodemo-Issyo are characters for Play Station games. Characters include Toro (drum and fife band), Toro (Afro), Toro (construction worker), Toro (rodeo), Toro, (soccer), and Kuro (soccer).

Loose:	**$20-$25 set**
With Packaging:	**$25-$30 set**
Vending card:	**$5-$10**

Vending card for the Dokodemo-Issyo 2 series.

Dokodemo-Issyo 2 (L to R): Toro (drum and fife band), Toro (Afro), Toro (construction worker), Toro (rodeo), Toro, (soccer), and Kuro (soccer).

Dragon Ball Z I

December 2005, With Feet

Dragon Ball Z is Japanese animation. Characters include Son Goku (Super Saiyan), Piccolo, Kuririn, Vegeta, and Freeza (First Form).

Loose:	**$15-$20 set**
With Packaging:	**$20-$25 set**
Vending card:	**$5-$10**

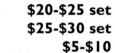

Vending card for the Dragon Ball Z Series I.

Dragon Ball Z Series I (L to R): Son Goku (Super Saiyan), Piccolo, Kuririn, Vegeta, and Freeza.

Dragon Ball Z 2

June 2006, With Feet

Dragon Ball Z is Japanese animation. Characters include Majin Buu, Mr. Satan, Son Goku, Son Gohan, and Gotenks (Super Saiyan).

Loose: $15-$20 set
With Packaging: $20-$25 set
Vending card: $5-$10

Dragon Ball Z Series 2 (L to R): Majin Buu, Mr. Satan, Son Goku, Son Gohan, and Gotenks (Super Saiyan).

Vending card for the Dragon Ball Z Series 2.

Dragon Ball Z 3

March 2007, With Feet

Dragon Ball Z is Japanese animation. Pictured L to R- Perfect Cell, Shenlong, Son Goku (Super Saiyan), Son Gohan (Super Saiyan), and Trunks (Super Saiyan).

Loose: $15-$20 set
With Packaging: $20-$25 set
Vending card: $5-$10

Dragon Ball Z Series 3 (L to R): Perfect Cell, Shenlong, Son Goku (Super Saiyan), Son Gohan (Super Saiyan) and Trunks (Super Saiyan).

Vending card for the Dragon Ball Z Series 3.

Final Fantasy

July 2005, With Feet

Final Fantasy is a role playing game. Characters include Knight, Samurai, Ryu-Kishi, Shiro Madoushi, and Toki-Madoushi.

Loose: $15-$20 set
With Packaging: $20-$25 set
Vending card: $5-$10

Final Fantasy (L to R): Knight, Samurai, Ryu-Kishi, Shiro Madoushi, and Toki-Madoushi.

Vending card for the Final Fantasy series.

Frog Style

October 2004, With Feet

Frogs are an original Bandai design. Characters include Green Frog, Yellow Frog, Orange Frog, Pink Frog, and Mizuiro Frog.

Loose:	$15-$20 set
With Packaging:	$20-$25 set
Vending card:	$5-$10

Vending card for the Frog Style series.

Frog Style (L to R): Green Frog, Yellow Frog, Orange Frog, Pink Frog, and Mizuiro Frog.

Frog Style Love Collection

September 2006, With Feet

Frogs are an original Bandai design. Characters include I (heart) PEZ Frog, Cupid Frog, Anniversary Frog, Love Frog, and Omelet Frog.

Loose:	$15-$20 set
With Packaging:	$20-$25 set
Vending card:	$5-$10

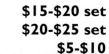

Vending card for the Frog Style Love Collection series.

Frog Style Love Collection (L to R): I (heart) PEZ Frog, Cupid Frog, Anniversary Frog, Love Frog, and Omelet Frog.

Gundam

2005, With Feet

Gundam is an animated series in Japan where the characters are space pilots who protect the earth from the evil Earth Sphere Alliance. Characters include Zaku 2 MS-06F, Char's Zaku MS-065, Gundam RX-78-2, and Z-Gock MSM-07.

Loose:	$5-$8 ea.
Mint in box:	$8-$10 ea.

Gundam loose (L to R): Zaku 2 MS-06F, Char's Zaku MS-065, Gundam RX-78-2, and Z-Gock MSM-07.

Gundam in box (L to R): Zaku 2 MS-06F, Char's Zaku MS-065, Gundam RX-78-2, and Z-Gock MSM-07.

Junior City 1 (L to R): J'aime Mint (Pom Ponette), Blue Berrie (Mezzo Piano), Key-Ko (Blue Cross girls), and Nakamura-Kun (Angel blue).

Junior City 1
April 2005, With Feet

Junior City is a children's clothing store in Japan, these are characters from several of the fashion brands including J'aime Mint (Pom Ponette), Blue Berrie (Mezzo Piano), Key-Ko (Blue Cross girls), and Nakamura-Kun (Angel blue).

Loose:	**$35-$40 set**
With Packaging:	**$40-$45 set**
Vending card:	**N/A**

Junior City 2 (L to R): Chibi-Zo (Blue Cross Girls), Hana-Chan (Angel Blue), Looky (Daisy Lovers), Lovely Berrie (Mezzo Piano), and I (Heart) Quu (Pom Ponette).

Junior City 2
March 2006, With Feet

Junior City is a children's clothing store in Japan, these are characters from several of the fashion brands including Chibi-Zo (Blue Cross Girls), Hana-Chan (Angel Blue), Looky (Daisy Lovers), Lovely Berrie (Mezzo Piano), and I (Heart) Quu (Pom Ponette).

Loose:	**$35-$40 set**
With Packaging:	**$40-$45 set**
Vending card:	**N/A**

Kamen Rider 1 (also known as Masked Rider)
March 2004, With Feet

Characters are from a Japanese science fiction story and include Shocker, Kamen Rider Amazon, Kamen Rider V3, Kamen Rider 2, and Kamen Rider 1 (old version).

Loose:	**$25-$30 set**
With Packaging:	**$30-$35 set**
Vending card:	**$5-$10**

Vending card for the Kamen Rider 1 (Masked Rider 1) series.

Kamen Rider 1 (L to R): Shocker, Kamen Rider Amazon, Kamen Rider V3, Kamen Rider 2, and Kamen Rider 1 (old version).

Kamen Rider 2 (also known as Masked Rider)

July 2004, With Feet

Characters are from a Japanese science fiction story and include Dokudahlian-Soldier, Bat-Man, Spider-Man, Rider Man, and Kamen Rider 1 (new version).

Loose:	**$15-$20 set**
With Packaging:	**$20-$25 set**
Vending card:	**$5-$10**

Vending card for the Kamen Rider 2 (Masked Rider 2) series.

Kamen Rider 2 (L to R): Dokudahlian-Soldier, Bat-Man, Spider-Man, Rider Man, and Kamen Rider 1 (new version).

Keroro Gunsou 1

July 2005, With Feet

Keroro Gunsou is based on Japanese animation. Characters include Sergeant Major Kururu, Private Tamama, Sergeant Keroro, Corporal Gioro, and Lance Corporal Dororo.

Loose:	**$15-$20 set**
With Packaging:	**$20-$25 set**
Vending card:	**$5-$10**

Vending card for the Keroro Gunsou 1 series.

Keroro Gunsou 1 (L to R): Sergeant Major Kururu, Private Tamama, Sergeant Keroro, Corporal Gioro, and Lance Corporal Dororo.

Keroro Gunsou 2

Febuary 2006, With Feet

Keroro Gunsou is based on Japanese animation. Characters include Corporal Giroro, Sergeant Keroro A, Sergeant Afro, Sergeant Keroro B, and Private Tamama.

Loose:	**$15-$20 set**
With Packaging:	**$20-$25 set**
Vending card:	**$5-$10**

Vending card for the Keroro Gunsou 2 series.

Keroro Gunsou 2 (L to R): Corporal Giroro, Sergeant Keroro A, Seargent Afro, Sergeant Keroro B, and Private Tamama.

Magi Ranger

Febuary 2006, With Feet

Special set sold as retail promotion and not in vending machines. Characters include Magi Green, Magi Pink, Magi Blue, Magi Red, and Magi Yellow.

Value: **$50-$60 in box**

The Magi Ranger series was not sold in vending machines, only in the box as shown.

JAPANESE

Mario Brothers

Febuary 2006, With Feet

Mario Brothers is a popular Nintendo video game. Characters include Toad, Yoshi, Wario, Donkey Kong, and Mario.

Loose:	$15-$20 set
With Packaging:	$20-$25 set
Vending card:	$5-$10

Mario Brothers (L to R): Toad, Yoshi, Wario, Donkey Kong, and Mario.

Vending card for the Mario Brothers series.

Moomin

April 2005, With Feet

Moomin are characters based on books in Finland. Characters include Moomin, Snork Maiden, Little My, Snufkin, and The Haifatteners.

Loose:	$15-$20 set
With Packaging:	$20-$25 set
Vending card:	$5-$10

Moomin (L to R): Moomin, Snork Maiden, Little My, Snufkin, and The Haifatteners.

Vending card for the Moomin series.

Oden-Kun

January 2007, With Feet

Oden-Kun characters are based on Japanese children's books and television animation. Characters include Ganguro-Tamago-Chan, Nise-Oden-Kun, Pero, Oden-Kun, and Tamago Chan.

Vending card for the Oden-Kun series.

Loose:	**$15-$20 set**
With Packaging:	**$20-$25 set**
Vending card:	**$5-$10**

Oden-Kun (L to R): Ganguro-Tamago-Chan, Nise-Oden-Kun, Pero, Oden-Kun, and Tamago Chan.

One Piece

Febuary 2006, With Feet

One Piece are characters based on Japanese animation and include Tony Tony Chopper, Going Merry, Monkey D Luffy, Nami, and Roronoa Zoro.

Vending card for the One Piece series.

Loose:	**$15-$20 set**
With Packaging:	**$20-$25 set**
Vending card:	**$5-$10**

One Piece (L to R): Tony Tony Chopper, Going Merry, Monkey D Luffy, Nami, and Roronoa Zoro.

Pingu

April 2004, With Feet

Pingu are Japanese clay animation characters including Robby, Pingu (tearful), Pingu (trumpet mouth), Pingu, and Pinga.

Vending card for the Pingu series.

Loose:	**$15-$20 set**
With Packaging:	**$20-$25 set**
Vending card:	**$5-$10**

Pingu (L to R): Robby, Pingu (tearful), Pingu (trumpet mouth), Pingu, and Pinga.

Pingu crystal variation

July 2006, With Feet

Pingu are Japanese clay animation characters including Pingu, Pingu (tearful), Pingu (trumpet mouth), Pinga, and Robby.

Loose: $15-$20 set
With Packaging: $20-$25 set
Vending card: $5-$10

Pingu Crystal Variation (L to R): Pingu, Pingu (tearful), Pingu (trumpet mouth), Pinga, and Robby.

Vending card for the Crystal Pingu series.

Pokémon 1

April 2004, With Feet

Pokémon are characters based on Japanese animation. This series includes Pikachu, Torchic, Treeco, Mudkip, and Jirachi.

Loose: $15-$20 set
With Packaging: $20-$25 set
Vending card: $5-$10

Pokémon 1 (L to R): Pikachu, Torchic, Treeco, Mudkip, and Jirachi.

Vending card for the Pokémon 1 series.

Pokémon 2

August 2004, With Feet

Pokémon are characters based on Japanese animation. Series 2 includes Deoxys, Gonbe, Meowth, Plusle, and Minun.

Loose: $15-$20 set
With Packaging: $20-$25 set
Vending card: $5-$10

Pokémon 2 (L to R): Deoxys, Gonbe, Meowth, Plusle, and Minun.

Vending card for the Pokémon 2 series.

Pokémon 3

October 2005, With Feet

Pokémon are characters based on Japanese animation. Series 3 includes Manene, Rukario, Pikachu, Mew, and Manyula.

Vending card for the Pokémon 3 series.

Loose:	**$15-$20 set**
With Packaging:	**$20-$25 set**
Vending card:	**$5-$10**

Pokémon 3 (L to R): Manene, Rukario, Pikachu, Mew, and Manyula.

Ponkickies 1 (also known as Gachapin)

July 2005, With Feet

Ponkickies are characters from an educational Japanese television series. Series 1 includes Gachapin (normal version), Mukku, Chibimimi, P-Chan, and Gachapin (diving version).

Vending card for the Ponkickies 1 (Gachapin 1) series.

Loose:	**$15-$20 set**
With Packaging:	**$20-$25 set**
Vending card:	**$5-$10**

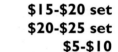

Ponkickies 1 (L to R): Gachapin (normal version), Mukku, Chibimimi, P-Chan, and Gachapin (diving version).

Ponkickies 2 (also known as Gachapin 2)

December 2005, With Feet

Ponkickies are characters from an educational Japanese television series. Series 2 includes Gachapin (diving version), Gachapin (normal version), Mukku, Chibimimi, and P-Chan.

Vending card for the Ponkickies 2 (Gachapin 2) series.

Loose:	**$15-$20 set**
With Packaging:	**$20-$25 set**
Vending card:	**$5-$10**

Ponkickies 2 (L to R): Gachapin (diving version), Gachapin (normal version), Mukku, Chibimimi, and P-Chan.

Rody

December 2004, With Feet

Rody is a child's rocking horse. Dispensers include Yellow Rody, Purple Rody, Red Rody, Blue Rody, and Cowboy.

Loose: $15-$20 set
With Packaging: $20-$25 set
Vending card: $5-$10

Rody (L to R): Yellow Rody, Purple Rody, Red Rody, Blue Rody, and Cowboy.

Vending card for the Rody series.

Rody Meets Frog Style

October 2005, With Feet

Rody is a child's rocking horse, Frog Style are characters created by Bandai. Dispensers include yellow Rody w/ red Frog, orange Rody w/ green Frog, green Rody w/purple Frog, red Rody w/yellow Frog, and Cowboy.

Loose: $15-$20 set
With Packaging: $20-$25 set
Vending card: $5-$10

Rody Meets Frog Style (L to R): yellow Rody w/ red Frog, orange Rody w/ green Frog, green Rody w/purple Frog, red Rody w/yellow Frog, and Cowboy.

Vending card for the Rody Meets Frog Style series.

San-X

November 2006, With Feet

San-X is a Japanese character for miscellaneous goods and stationery. Characters include Relakkuma, Nyan-Nyan-Nyanko, Mamegoma, Tsuginohi-Kerori, Monokuro Boo White, and Monokuro Boo Black. This came in a set of 5, with either the white pig or the black pig.

Loose: $15-$20 set
With Packaging: $20-$25 set
Vending card: $5-$10

San-X (L to R): Relakkuma, Nyan- Nyan-Nyanko, Mamegoma, Tsuginohi-Kerori, Monokuro Boo White, and Monokuro Boo Black.

Vending card for the San-X series.

Tamagocchi

March 2006, With Feet

Tamagocchi are characters for mobile games. Characters include Mamecchi, Kuchipacchi, Memecchi, Fulawacchi, and Mimicchi.

Vending card for the Tamagocchi series.

Loose:	**$15-$20 set**
With Packaging:	**$20-$25 set**
Vending card:	**$5-$10**

Tamagocchi (L to R): Mamecchi, Kuchipacchi, Memecchi, Fulawacchi, and Mimicchi.

Thomas and Friends

May 2004, With Feet

Thomas the Tank is based on an animated train character from a British children's television series. Characters include Percy (#6), James (#5), Gordon (#4), Henry (#3), Edward (#2), and Thomas (#1).

Vending card for the Thomas and Friends series.

Loose:	**$30-$35 set**
With Packaging:	**$35-$40 set**
Vending card:	**$5-$10**

Thomas and Friends (L to R): Percy (#6), James (#5), Gordon (#4), Henry (#3), Edward (#2), and Thomas (#1).

Ultraman 1

March 2004, With Feet

Japanese animation heroes. Characters include Ultraman, Ultraman Seven, Ultraman Tiga, Ultraman Cosmos (Eclipse Mode), and Baltan.

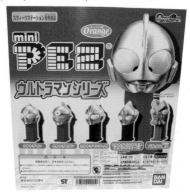

Vending card for the Ultraman 1 series.

Loose:	**$30-$35 set**
With Packaging:	**$35-$40 set**
Vending cards:	**$5-$10**

Ultraman 1 (L to R): Ultraman, Ultraman Seven, Ultraman Tiga, Ultraman Cosmos (Eclipse Mode), and Baltan.

Ultraman 2

September 2004, With Feet

Japanese animation heroes. Characters include Dada, Ace Killer, Ultraman Ace, Ultraman Taro, and Ultraman Dyna.

Loose: $15-$20 set
With Packaging: $20-$25 set
Vending cards: $5-$10

Ultraman 2 (L to R): Dada, Ace Killer, Ultraman Ace, Ultraman Taro, and Ultraman Dyna.

Vending card for the Ultraman 2 series.

Ultraman 3

November 2004, With Feet

Japanese animation heroes. Characters include Ultraman Nexus (Junis Mode), Ultraman Nexus (Anphans mode), Ultraman Leo, Busuka, and Kanegon.

Loose: $15-$20 set
With Packaging: $20-$25 set
Vending cards: $5-$10

Ultraman 3 (L to R): Ultraman Nexus (Junis Mode), Ultraman Nexus (Anphans mode), Ultraman Leo, Busuka, and Kanegon.

Vending card for the Ultraman 3 series.

Zenmai-Zamurai

Febuary 2007, With Feet

Zenmai-Zamurai are characters based on Japanese animation. Characters include Zenmai-Zamurai, Mamemaru, Zukin-Chan, Botan-Chan, and Maccha.

Loose: $15-$20 set
With Packaging: $20-$25 set
Vending cards: $5-$10

L to R- Zenmai-Zamurai, Mamemaru, Zukin-Chan, Botan-chan, and Maccha.

Vending card for the Zenmai-Zamurai series.

Annie
Early 1980s, No Feet

Released to coincide with the release of the movie *Annie*. The movie wasn't a hit and neither was the dispenser, making this one a little tough to find.

Value: $125-$150

Asterix is a popular European comic. These dispensers have not been released in the U.S. The series was first produced by PEZ in the mid-1970s and a remake of the original series was released in the late 1990s. The remakes have feet and painted on eyes. The Roman Soldier was not included in the original series.

Asterix
Mid-1970s, No Feet and With Feet

Original:	$1500-$2000
Remake:	$3-$5

Muselix
Mid-1970s, No Feet and With Feet

Original:	$2500-$3000
Remake, called "Getafix" by PEZ:	$3-$5

Obelix
Mid-1970s, No Feet and With Feet

Original:	$1500-$2000
Remake:	$3-$5

Roman Soldier
Late 1990s, With Feet

Value:	$3-$5

Asterix series, originally released in the mid-1970s. (L to R): Asterix, Muselix, Obelix.

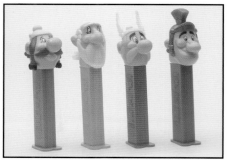

Remake of the Asterix series. (L to R): Obelix, Muselix (sometimes called "Getafix" in European ads), Asterix, and Roman Soldier.

Bob the Builder
2002, With Feet

Value: $1-$2

Scoop from the Bob the Builder series.

Bob the Builder series released in 2002: Bob, Wendy, Pilchard the Cat, and Spud the Scarecrow.

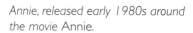

Annie, released early 1980s around the movie Annie.

Bozo the Clown

Early 1960s, No Feet

This dispenser is usually die-cut on the side of the stem with a picture of Bozo and Butch. The non-die-cut stem is actually more difficult to find.

Die-cut Stem:	**$175-$200**
Plain Stem:	**$185-$200**

Bozo the Clown, from the early 1960s.

Bratz

2005, With Feet

Cloe, Jade, Yasmine, and Sasha.

Value:	**$1-$2**
Yellow Eye Sasha:	**$15-$20**

Bratz (L-R): Cloe, Jade, Yasmine, and Sasha.

A hard to find, non-USA, yellow eye version of Sasha.

Bullwinkle

Early 1960s, No Feet

Bullwinkle can be found with either a yellow or a brown stem—the brown is much harder to find.

Yellow Stem:	**$250-$275**
Brown Stem:	**$275-$325**

Bullwinkle, from the early 1960s. The brown stem version on the right is much harder to find than the yellow stem version.

Casper

Late 1950s, No Feet

It's hard to say for sure which licensed character first graced the top of a PEZ dispenser. Some say it was Mickey Mouse, some say Popeye, and others say Casper. One story as told by Mr. Curt Allina, executive vice-president of PEZ from 1953 to1979, was that he and Mr. Harvey, creator of Casper and Harvey Comics, had apartments in the same New York building in the 1950s. While living there the two developed a friendship and an agreement to use Harvey's character on the candy dispenser. Casper can be found with white, light blue, and light yellow stems as well as a die-cut version with a red or black sleeve.

Value: **$150-$175**

Die-cut Stem: **$200-$250**

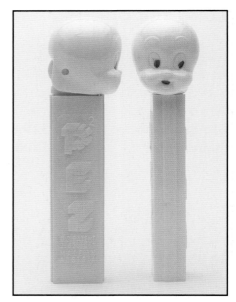

Harvey Cartoon character Casper the Friendly Ghost, from the late 1950s.

Elvis

2007, With Feet

The 30th anniversary of Elvis' death occurred in 2007. PEZ issued a set of three dispensers, one from each of his most popular decades to commemorate Elvis' long career. A special three-song sampler CD is included in the set. Songs include "Hound Dog" from 1956, "Follow That Dream" from 1961, and "The Wonder of You" from 1970. Limited to 400,000, each tin is individually numbered with a hologram sticker.

Value: **$20-$25**

E.T.

2002, With Feet

Value: $2-$4

The king of rock and roll is now a PEZ dispenser! Thank you— thank you very much.

Phone home, it's E.T.! Came out with the summer 2002 movie re-release.

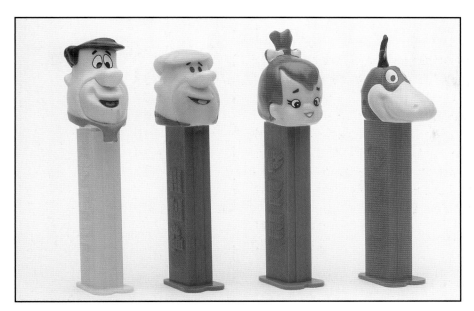

Flintstones

Mid-1990s, With Feet

Series includes Barney Rubble, Dino, Fred Flintstone, and Pebbles Flintstone.

Value: $1-$2

That modern stone-age family—The Flintstones. (L to R): Fred, Barney, Pebbles, and Dino.

Garfield

1990s, With Feet

Two series featuring the comic strip character Garfield have been produced—the first in the early 1990s, the second in the late 1990s. The first series includes Garfield, Garfield with teeth, Garfield with visor, Arlene, and Nermal. The second series includes Garfield, Chef Garfield, Sleepy Garfield, Aviator Garfield, and Odie.

First Series: $2-$3 each

Second Series: $1-$2 each

Garfield 1st Series. (L to R): Garfield, Garfield with teeth, Garfield with visor, Arlene, and Nermal (two versions).

Garfield 2nd Series. (L to R): Garfield, Chef Garfield, Sleepy Garfield, Aviator Garfield, and Odie.

A rare test mold version of Garfield.

A rare, clear version of Garfield.

Another rare version of Garfield, this one is mounted on a Euro card.

Hello Kitty

2005 to current, With Feet

Characters include Hello Kitty, My Melody, Chococat, and Kuririn.

USA Version (2005):	**$1-$2**
Crystal Heads (2006):	**$2-$4**
Crystal Heads w/stenciled stems (2006):	**$3-$4**
Crystal Head Collectors Tin (2006):	**$8-$10**
Japanese Version (2007):	**$3-$4**
Chococat (2007):	**$1-$2**

Chococat from the Hello Kitty series.

Hello Kitty metal gift tin or lunch box featuring 4 crystal head dispensers.

Hello Kitty crystal head with stenciled stems (L to R): Hello Kitty, My Melody, Kuririn, and Hello Kitty w/rabbit. (Non-USA).

Hello Kitty USA versions (L to R): Aloha Kitty, Hello Kitty w/rabbit, Hello Kitty, and My Melody.

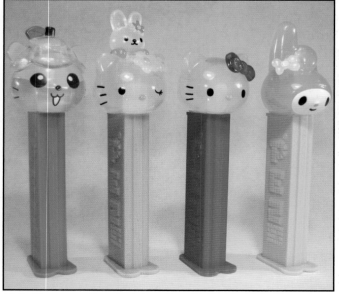

Hello Kitty crystal head versions (L to R): Kuririn, Hello Kitty w/ rabbit, Hello Kitty, and My Melody. (Non-USA).

Ice Age 2

2006, With Feet

Characters from the 20th Century Fox animated adventure *Ice Age 2: The Meltdown* include Scrat, Manny, Diego, and Sid.

Value: $1-$2

Ice Age 2 (L to R): Scrat, Manny, Diego, and Sid.

Kyoro-Chan

2007, With Feet

Kyoro-Chan is a Japanese bird that serves as a mascot for Chocoball, a brand of chocolate made by the Morinaga company. He had his own animae series in the late '90s plus a Nintendo video game.

Value: $3-$4

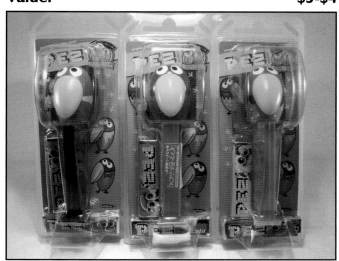

The Chocoball mascot—Kyoro-Chan.

Madagascar

2005, With Feet

Characters from the DreamWorks animated feature film *Madagascar* include Marty the zebra (2 different eye variations), Gloria the hippo, and Alex the lion (one version has a painted line under his nose, the other does not). Skipper the penguin is pictured on display boxes but never went into production.

Value: $1-$2

Madagascar (L to R): Marty the zebra (2 different eye variations), Gloria the hippo, and Alex the lion (line and no line under the nose variations).

Mr. Bean

2005, With Feet

A set of four dispensers including Mr. Bean's car the Mini Cooper, Mr. Bean, Irma Gobb, and Teddy.

Value: $1-$2

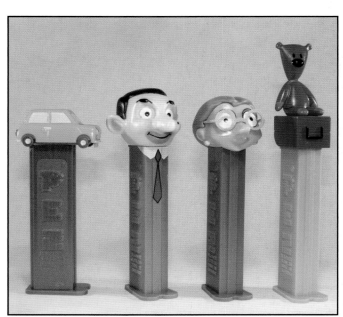

Mr. Bean (L to R): Mini Cooper, Mr. Bean, Irma Gobb, and Teddy.

MGM Characters

Barney Bear

Early 1980s, No Feet and With Feet

No Feet:	$35-$45
With Feet:	$20-$30

Barney Bear, an MGM character released in the early 1980s.

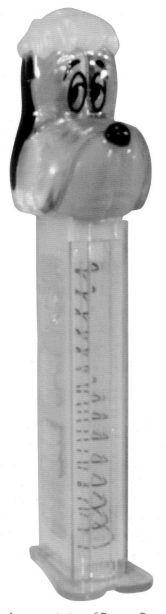

Droopy

Early 1980s, No Feet and With Feet

This dispenser was not released in the U.S. Two versions were made—one with painted ears and one with movable ears.

Painted ears:	$3-$8
Moveable ears:	$20-$25

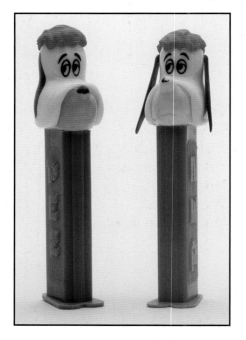

Droopy, an MGM character released in the early 1980s but not in the U.S.

A rare variation of Droopy Dog.

Jerry

Early 1980s to current, No Feet and With Feet

One half of MGM's famous cat and mouse duo. Not released in the U.S. There are MANY variations of this dispenser.

No Feet:	$30-$40
Thin Feet:	$5-$10
Multi-piece face:	$10-$15
With Feet:	$4-$8
Current:	$2-$3

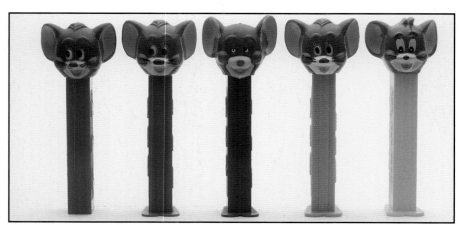

Jerry, from the early 1980s to current. (L to R): No Feet, Thin Feet, Multi-Piece Face, With Feet, and the Current release.

Rare ear insert versions of Jerry and Tuffy.

Variations of the multi-piece face Jerry.

Spike

Early 1980s, No Feet and With Feet
Spike was not released in the U.S. Several versions exist including small painted eyes, decal eyes, and an unusual variation with a green head.

Decal eyes:	**$5-$10**
Small painted eyes:	**$15-$20**
Green head:	**$125-$150**

Tom

Early 1980s, No Feet and With Feet
The feline portion of MGM's famous cat and mouse pair. Not released in the U.S. Several versions have been produced.

No Feet:	**$25-$35**
With Feet:	**$3-$8**
Multi-piece face:	**$5-$10**

Spike, an MGM character released in the early 1980s. Decal eye version on the left is more common.

Tom, an MGM character first released in the early 1980s.

Tuffy

Early 1990s, With Feet
A non-U.S. release, Tuffy looks similar to Jerry but has gray face instead of brown.

Painted Face:	**$3-$5**
Multi-piece face:	**$10-$15**
Current:	**$2-$4**

Tuffy, an MGM character first released in the early 1990s.

Tyke

Early 1980s, No Feet and With Feet
Non-U.S. release.

Small Painted Eyes:	**$25-$35**
Decal Eyes:	**$15-$20**

Tyke, an MGM character first released in the early 1980s. Printed eye version on the right is more common.

Muppets

Early 1990s, With Feet

Included in the series are Fozzie Bear, Gonzo, Kermit the Frog, and Miss Piggy. A harder to find version with eyelashes exists of Miss Piggy.

Miss Piggy with eyelashes: $10-$15

Miss Piggy (common and current versions): $1-$3

Fozzie, Gonzo, and Kermit: $1-$2

Kermit, Fozzie Bear, and Gonzo from the Muppets series.

Miss Piggy from the Muppets. (L to R): "Eyelash" Version, Common "A" Version, and version "B."

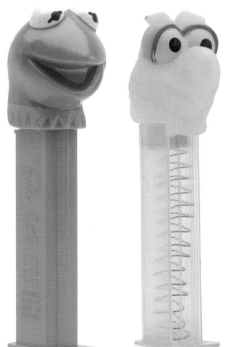

Rare Gonzo test mold variation.

Newest version of Kermit the Frog.

Nintendo

Late 1990s, With Feet

A series not available in the U.S. featuring characters from Nintendo's video games. Dispensers include Diddy Kong, Yoshi, Koopa Trooper, and Mario.

Value: $2-$3 each

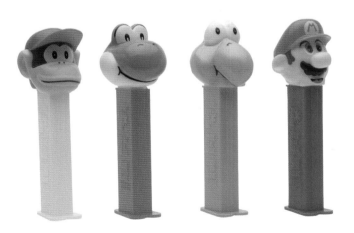

Nintendo series. (L to R): Diddy Kong, Yoshi, Koopa Trooper, and Mario.

Open Season

2006, With Feet

Characters from the Sony Pictures animated film include Elliot, Mr. Weenie, Boog, and McSquizzy.

Value: **$1-$2**

Open Season (L to R): Elliot (deer), Mr. Weenie (daschund), Boog (bear), and McSquizzy (squirrel).

Orange County Choppers (OCC)

2006, With Feet

Paul Sr., Paul Jr., and Mikey are immortalized as PEZ dispensers! This set marks the first time PEZ has put a living person on top of its world famous candy dispenser. 300,000 of these sets were produced and sold out almost immediately.

Value: **$10-$15**

The first living people to be made into PEZ dispensers—the Teutul's of Orange County Choppers.

Over the Hedge

2006, With Feet

Characters from the DreamWorks animated film *Over the Hedge* include Stella, Verne, RJ, and Hammy.

Value: **$1-$2**

Over the Hedge (L to R): Stella the skunk, Verne the turtle, RJ the raccoon, and Hammy the squirrel.

Peanuts Characters

Peanuts

Early 1990s to current, With Feet

Characters include Charlie Brown, Lucy, Snoopy, Woodstock, and Peppermint Patty. Several variations exist for each.

Charlie Brown, smiling:	**$1-$2**
Charlie Brown, frowning (non-U.S.):	**$15-$20**
Charlie Brown, tongue showing (non-U.S.):	**$15-$20**
Charlie Brown, eyes closed (non-U.S.):	**$50-$60**
Lucy, common version:	**$1-$2**
Lucy, white around eyes:	**$50-$75**
Lucy, white face (known as "Psycho Lucy"):	**$75-$90**
Peppermint Patty:	**$1-$2**
Snoopy:	**$1-$3**
Snoopy as "Joe Cool":	**$1-$3**
Woodstock, common version:	**$1-$2**
Woodstock with feathers (black markings on the top and back of his head):	**$3-$5**

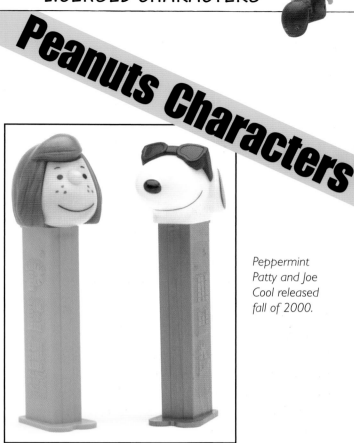

Peppermint Patty and Joe Cool released fall of 2000.

Lucy from the Peanuts series. (L to R): Common Version, White around Eyes, White Face (Psycho Lucy).

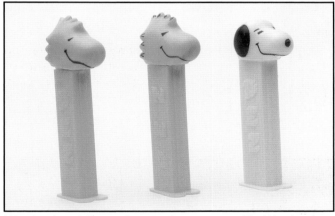

Woodstock and Snoopy from the Peanuts series. The Woodstock with Feathers is in the center. (Non-U.S. release).

Peanuts 2000. (L to R): Charlie Brown, Lucy, Snoopy, and Woodstock.

Charlie Brown from the Peanuts series. (L to R): Smiling, Frowning, With Tongue Showing.

Peter PEZ

Late 1970s, No Feet and With Feet
A dispenser featuring the clown mascot of the PEZ Candy company. The original was produced in the late 1970s and a remake came out in the early 1990s.

Original version, No Feet:	**$50-$75**
Remake (1993 to 2001):	**$2-$4**
Current:	**$1-$2**
"Rico" variation:	**$20-$30**

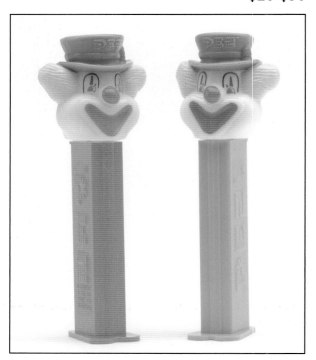

2001 version "B" of Peter PEZ. Dispenser on the left glows in the dark (mail order only).

Peter PEZ "Rico" variation. "Rico" means candy.

Peter PEZ, originally appeared in the late 1970s. The original version is on the left, and the remake "A" from the 1990s is on the right.

A hard to find variation of Peter Pez.

Pink Panther

Late 1990s, With Feet

Not available in the U.S., this series featured the Pink Panther, Inspector Clousseau, Ant, and Aardvark.

Value: $3-$4 each

2002 remake "Pinky" Pink Panther: $5-$10

2002 version of Pink Panther also known as "Pinky" Pink Panther.

Pink Panther series, released in the late 1990s. (L to R): Pink Panther, Inspector Clouseau, Ant, and Aardvark.

Pokémon

2001, With Feet

Value: $3-$4

Pokémon dispensers released in 2001. (L to R): Pikachu, Meowth, Mew, Psyduck, and Koffing.

Popeye

Late 1950s to late 1970s, No Feet
Some believe Popeye was the first licensed character PEZ ever used on a dispenser. Brutus and Olive Oyl were produced in the mid-1960s and usually are found with missing or chipped paint on their faces.

Popeye, original version, hat is molded to the head:	**$150-$175**
Popeye B, plain face:	**$125-$150**
Popeye C, with pipe (note the pipe is the same piece used on Mickey Mouse's nose):	**$100-$125**
Brutus:	**$250-$275**
Olive Oyl:	**$275-$325**

Brutus and Olive Oyl, from the mid-1960s.

Popeye, from the late 1950s to late 1970s. (L to R): Original version with hat molded to head (2 examples), Version B, Version C with removable pipe (2 examples).

Sesame Street

2005, With Feet and No Feet
PEZ also offered collectors versions of Big Bird, Elmo and Cookie Monster on their web site that came packaged in special boxes celebrating the 35th anniversary of Sesame Street. The no foot version was only offered on the special limited edition set.

Value:	**$1-$2**
35th Anniversary box set:	**$30-$45**

Sesame Street (L to R): Cookie Monster, Zoe, Bert, Ernie, Elmo, and Big Bird.

35th anniversary box set, only available through a PEZ mail order offer.

Shrek

2004, With Feet
Initially only released in Europe, it wasn't until 2007 that you could find Shrek in the United States.

Value:	**$1-$2**
Silver Donkey (European movie promo):	**$15-$20**

Shrek (L to R): Shrek, Ogress Fiona, Puss 'n Boots, Donkey, and silver Donkey.

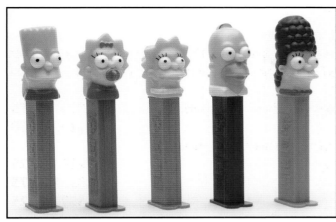

Smurfs

Late 1980s, No Feet and With Feet

Two Smurf series were produced—one in the late 1980s and the second in the late 1990s. Series one included Smurf, Smurfette, and Papa Smurf. The second series includes Smurf, Papa Smurf, Smurfette, Brainy Smurf, and Gargamel.

Smurf (1st series):	**$10-$15**
Smurfette (1st series):	**$10-$15**
Papa Smurf (1st series):	**$10-$15**
Second Series:	**$3-$5 each**

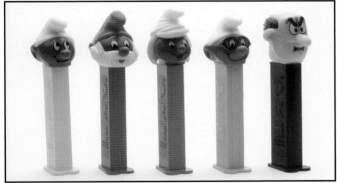

Smurfs, current series, released late 1990s. (L to R): Smurf, Papa Smurf, Smurfette, Brainy Smurf, and Gargamel.

Simpsons

Summer 2000, With Feet

D'oh! It's the whole Simpson family! Bart, Maggie, Lisa, Homer, and Marge.

Value: $1-$2 each

The Simpsons, released summer of 2000. (L to R): Bart, Maggie, Lisa, Homer, and Marge.

Smurfs, original series from the late 1980s including Smurf, Papa Smurf, and Smurfette.

Sponge Bob Square Pants

2004, With Feet

Value: $1-$2

Bob in his underwear: $2-$4

Sponge Bob Square Pants (L to R): Squidward, Sponge Bob, Sponge Bob in his underwear, and Patrick.

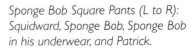

Star Wars

Late 1990s to current, With Feet

PEZ released four series of dispensers featuring characters from the *Star Wars* universe. The first series included five dispensers: Darth Vader, Stormtrooper, C3-PO, Yoda, and Chewbacca. The second series, released summer of 1999 included: Ewok, Princess Leia, Boba Fett, and Luke Skywalker. The third series released summer 2002 in conjunction with the movie *Attack of the Clones* featured Jango Fett, R2-D2, and Clone Trooper. The fourth series, released summer of 2005 includes; New Chewbacca, Death Star planet, Emperor Palpatine (regular version, Emperor Palpatine glow in the dark version is exclusive to Wal-Mart), and General Grievous. The 2005 collector's edition box sets can be found in two different variations, one for Wal-Mart and one for all other retailers. Limited to a run of 250,000 sets, each was individually numbered and included nine dispensers and twelve packs of candy.

Value (all series):	**$1-$3 each**
Glowing Emperor Palpatine:	**$3-$5**
Box sets with nine dispensers:	**$15-$20**
Limited Edition sets (mail order offer from PEZ):	**$35-$50**

Jango Fett, R2-D2, and Clone Trooper. R2-D2 is only the second dispenser to have the entire body on top of the dispenser!

Star Wars (L to R): Chewbacca, General Grievous, Emperor Palpatine (regular version), Emperor Palpatine (glow in the dark version for Wal-Mart), and the Death Star.

Star Wars (L to R). Top Row: Stormtrooper, Darth Vader, Stormtrooper. Center Row: Ewok, Princess Leia, Boba Fett, Yoda. Bottom Row: Luke Skywalker, Chewbacca, C-3P0.

Numbered limited edition Star Wars set.

Back view of the Star Wars limited edition set.

Numbered limited edition Star Wars set done exclusively for Wal-Mart.

Star Wars special limited edition versions only available through a PEZ mail-order offer.

A rare version of Darth Vader mounted on a "halo" card.

Teenage Mutant Ninja Turtles

Mid-1990s, With Feet

Two series were produced—a smiling version and an angry version of Leonardo, Michelangelo, Donatello, and Raphael. With eight different turtle heads and eight stem colors, collecting all variations presents a bit of a challenge.

Smiling version:	**$2-$3 each**
Angry version:	**$2-$3 each**
2005 remakes:	**$1-$2 each**

Teenage Mutant Ninja Turtles—Smiling Version. (L to R): Leonardo, Michelangelo, Donatello, and Raphael.

Teenage Mutant Ninja Turtles—Grimacing Version. (L to R): Leonardo, Michelangelo, Donatello, and Raphael.

2005 remakes (L to R): Raphael, Michelangelo, Leonardo, and Donatello.

Tweenies

2002, With Feet

Released in Europe summer of 2002.

Value:
$2-$4 each

Tweenies released summer of 2002. (L to R): Jake, Fizz, Milo, Bella, and Doodles. These were the first actual dispensers to have stenciled stems!

Back in Action, Looney Tunes

2004, With Feet European Release.
Value: $3-$5

Looney Tunes Back in Action (L to R): Western Yosemite Sam, African Taz, French Tweety, Western Bugs, and Movie Director Daffy.

Cool Cat

Early 1980s, No Feet and With Feet

No Feet:	**$65-$85**
With Feet:	**$45-$65**
Pink:	**$800-$1000**

Bugs Bunny

Late 1970s to current, No Feet and With Feet

No Feet:	**$15-$20**
With Feet, older style head:	**$5-$10**
Painted Ears:	**$1-$2**
Current:	**$1-$2**

Bugs Bunny, from the late 1970s to current. (L to R): No feet, With feet and older style head (2 examples), Painted ears, and Current style.

A rare pink variation of Cool Cat.

Cool Cat, a Warner Brothers character, released in the early 1980s.

Daffy Duck

Late 1970s to current, No Feet and With Feet
Many versions of Daffy have been produced. The first version with separate eye pieces is the toughest to find.

Daffy Duck A (separate eye pieces): $25-$30
**Daffy Duck B (painted eyes
and tongue):** $15-$20
**Daffy Duck C (with feet, older
style head):** $5-$8
Daffy Duck D (current style): $1-$2

Daffy Duck, from the late 1970s to current. The version on the far left is toughest to find with the separate eye pieces.

Foghorn Leghorn

Early 1980s, No Feet and With Feet
Foghorn Leghorn can be found with either a yellow or an orange beak.

No Feet: $75-$95
With Feet: $65-$85

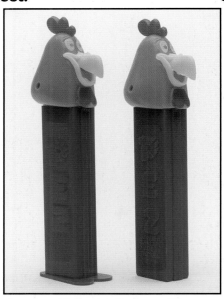

I say, I say it's Foghorn Leghorn, a Warner Brothers character, from the early 1980s.

Henry Hawk

Early 1980s, No Feet and With Feet

No Feet: $75-$85
With Feet: $60-$75

Henry Hawk, a Warner Brothers character, released in the early 1980s.

Merlin Mouse

Early 1980s, No Feet and With Feet

No Feet: $20-$30
With Feet: $12-$15

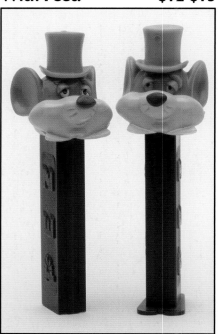

Merlin Mouse, a Warner Brothers character, from the early 1980s.

Petunia Pig

Early 1980s, No Feet and With Feet

No Feet: $40-$50
With Feet: $30-$40

Petunia Pig, a Warner Brothers character, dispenser first appeared in the early 1980s.

Roadrunner

Early 1980s, No Feet and With Feet

Painted eyes, No Feet:	**$30-$40**
Painted eyes, With Feet:	**$25-$30**
Stencil eyes, With Feet (this is the most common version):	**$20-$25**

Roadrunner, Warner Brothers character, from the early 1980s.

Sylvester

Late 1970s, No Feet and With Feet
Several versions of Tweety Bird's nemesis exist.

No Feet:	**$15-$20**
With Feet, older style head:	**$5-$8**
With Feet, with whiskers (black lines under nose), non-U.S. version:	**$4-$8**
Currents:	**$1-$2**

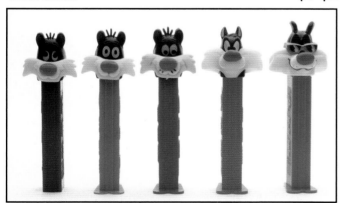

Sylvester, a Warner Brothers character, first released in the late 1970s. (L to R): No feet, With feet and older style head, With feet and whiskers (black lines under nose), Current (2 variations).

Speedy Gonzales

Late 1970s to current, No Feet and With Feet

No Feet:	**$30-$40**
With Feet, older head:	**$15-$25**
Current:	**$1-$2**

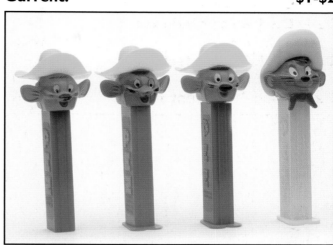

Speedy Gonzales, a Warner Brothers character, from the late 1970s to current.

Tazmanian Devil

Late 1990s, With Feet

Common Version:	**$1-$2**
Cycling Taz (with hat):	**$1-$2**

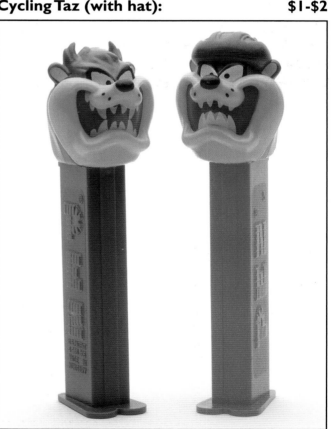

Tazmanian Devil and cycling Taz, released late 1990s.

Tweety

Late 1970s to Current, No Feet and With Feet
The oldest version is hardest to find; it has separate pieces for the eyes (known as removable eyes).

Removable eyes, No Feet:	**$20-$25**
Painted eyes, No Feet:	**$15-$20**
Painted eyes, With Feet:	**$3-$5**
Current:	**$1-$2**

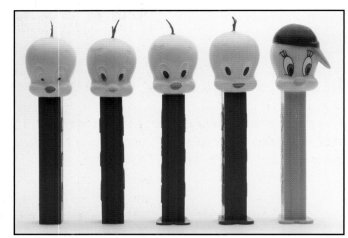

Tweety, a Warner Brothers character, first appeared in the late 1970s to current. The version on the far left is hardest to find. It has separate pieces for the eyes (known as removable eyes).

Wile E. Coyote

Early 1980s, No Feet and With Feet

No Feet:	**$45-$65**
With Feet:	**$35-$45**

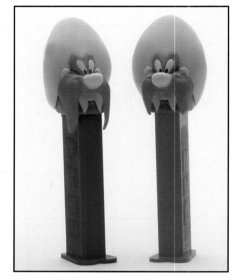

Yosemite Sam

Mid 1990s, With Feet
The shorter mustache on the non-U.S. version allows body parts to put on the dispenser.

U.S. Version:	**$1-$2**
Non-U.S. Version:	**$2-$4**

Yosemite Sam, a Warner Brothers character, released in the mid-1990s. The U.S. version is on the left. The short mustache version (European) was done to accommodate body parts, the long mustache would have been in the way.

Sport Looney Tunes

2006, With Feet
European Release.

Value:	**$3-$4**

Wile E. Coyote, a Warner Brothers character, first appeared in the early 1980s.

Sport Looney Tunes soccer balls.

Sport Looney Tunes (L to R): Bugs Bunny, Tweety Bird, and Tazmanian Devil.

Eerie Spectres (Also known as Soft-head Monsters)

Late 1970s, No Feet

This group is very popular among collectors. There are two variations for each character—"Made in Hong Kong" and "Hong Kong." These are the two different markings used on the back of the head with the "Hong Kong" mark being a bit harder to find. There is also a very distinct difference in face color between the two. The stems of these dispensers are always marked "Made in the USA." The six characters in the series are Air Spirit, Diabolic, Scarewolf, Spook, Vamp, and Zombie.

| "Made in Hong Kong": | $200-$225 |
| "Hong Kong": | $225-$250 |

Air Spirit (made in Hong Kong version is on the left).

Identifying marks on the back of the head.

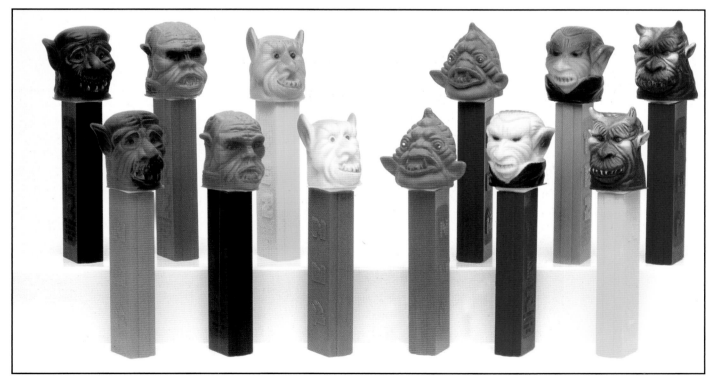

Eerie Specters, also known as "soft-head" monsters. These are from the late 1970s and very popular among collectors. There are two variations; "Made in Hong Kong" and "Hong Kong." The latter of the two is a bit harder to find. There is also a very distinct difference in face color between the two. The back row is the "Hong Kong" version. The stems of these dispensers are always marked, "Made in the USA."

Diabolic (made in Hong Kong version is on the left).

Spook (made in Hong Kong version is on the left).

Scarewolf (made in Hong Kong version is on the left).

Vamp (made in Hong Kong version is on the left).

Zombie (made in Hong Kong version is on the left).

Notice the difference in heads. These were painted by hand and can vary greatly in detail.

Fishman

Mid-1970s, No Feet

The Fishman used the same mold as the Creature from the Black Lagoon, which was done as part of a Universal Studios Monsters series. The Creature was all green whereas the Fishman came with either a green or a black head and various colored stems.

Value: $175-$200

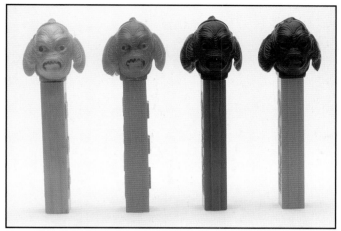

The all green version on the far left is known as the Creature from the Black Lagoon, or just the Creature. The others are referred to as the "Fishman." The Creature, from the mid-1960s, has a very unique "pearl-essant" stem that matches the head.

Mr. Ugly

Early 1970s, No Feet and With Feet

This really is a homely guy! Several variations to the face coloring exist and differ in value.

Chartreuse green face:	**$75-$95**
Aqua green face:	**$80-$90**
Olive green face:	**$60-$75**
With Feet:	**$45-$65**

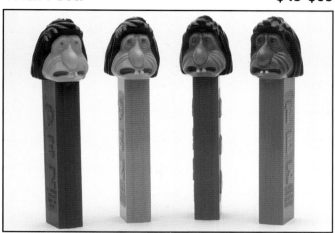

Mr. Ugly, from the early 1970s, with several head-color variations. (L to R): chartreuse green, aqua-green, and olive green.

One-Eyed Monster

Early 1970s, No Feet and With Feet

This dispenser was available with either an orange, brown, black, gray, pink, or yellow head. Black and gray are the harder colors to find and usually sell for a little more than the other variations. CAUTION: Reproductions or fakes surfaced in 2007 of this dispenser. When buying it is always best to purchase from a reputable dealer who will stand behind what he sells. The fakes have been somewhat difficult to distinguish from an original. Subtle mold flaws and differences in the plastic itself are the key clues when trying to determine what is original and what is a fake.

A selection of One Eye Monsters.

No Feet:	**$80-$100**
With Feet:	**$65-$80**
Black or	
Gray head:	**$100-$150**

One Eye Monster, from the early 1970s. Can also be found with brown, gray, pink, or yellow head. Watch out for fakes!

Universal Studios Monsters

Mid-1960s, No Feet

A highly coveted series among PEZ collectors and Universal Studio fans. The Creature has a very unique pearlescent stem.

Creature from the Black Lagoon:	**$300-$350**
Wolfman:	**$275-$300**
Frankenstein:	**$250-$300**

Universal Studios Monsters, from the mid-1960s. (L to R): Wolfman, Creature from the Black Lagoon, and Frankenstein.

PEZ Pals are one of my favorite groups. They are popular among collectors and have a clever concept to boot! Pezi Boy is a detective who dresses up in disguises to solve mysteries. With these various disguises he becomes different characters such as a Policeman, Knight, Sheik, and Doctor. These characters were shown in the Pezi comics—inserts that came packaged with the dispensers in the 1960s.

The characters all used the same head, so the PEZ Company only needed to produce small, inexpensive accessories to make a whole new dispenser. Kids were encouraged to "collect them all" and interchange the pieces to make their own character. It is easy to understand why many of these dispensers are missing parts.

Admiral
Date Unknown, No Feet
A very rare dispenser. The Admiral character has been shown on various PEZ advertisements such as comics and candy boxes but none had been found until a few years ago. This is the only one currently known to exist.

Value: $5000+

Alpine Man
Early 1970s, No Feet
Produced for the 1972 Munich Olympics, this is a very rare and difficult dispenser to find.

Green Hat: $2000+
Brown Hat: $3000+

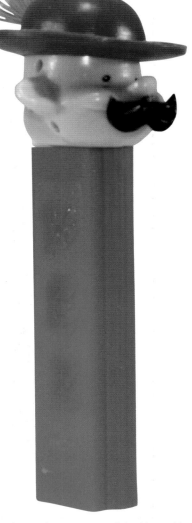

Admiral. A very rare dispenser, this is the only one currently known to exist.

Alpine Man, from the 1972 Munich Olympics.

A rare brown hat variation of the Alpine Man.

Boy and Boy with Cap

Mid-1960s-current, No Feet and With Feet

Many versions of the PEZ Pal Boy have been produced through the years. One of the rarest is the brown-hair boy without hat used in a mid-1980s promotion for the movie *Stand By Me*. The dispenser is packaged with one pack of multi-flavor candy and a miniature version of the movie poster announcing the videocassette release and the quote "If I could only have one food to eat for the rest of my life? That's easy, PEZ. Cherry flavored PEZ. No question about it." This dispenser must be sealed in original bag to be considered complete. For the Boy with Cap dispensers, watch for reproduction red hats. The reproduction hats have a slight a texture and little different sheen than an original.

Boy with blue cap, blonde hair:	**$85-$100**
Boy with red cap, blonde hair:	**$250-$300**
(watch for reproduction hats!)	
Boy with blue cap, brown hair:	**$75-$90**
Blonde Hair:	**$35-$45**
Brown Hair:	**$25-$35**
Stand By Me (sealed in bag with mini-poster):	**$150-$200**

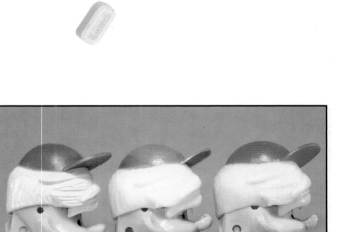

Promotional item for the 1986 movie Stand By Me.

Boy and Boy with Cap, from the mid-1960s. Both the blonde and brown-hair versions can also be found with a red hat.

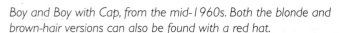

Different hair molds of the Boy with Cap dispenser.

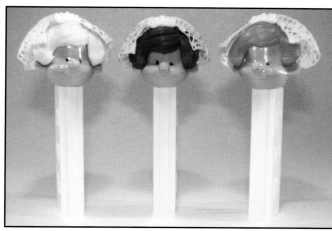

Blonde, brown, and red hair versions of the hard to find Bride.

Bride

Late 1970s, No Feet

The Bride is a very rare and much desired piece by collectors. This dispenser, along with the Groom, was created for Robert and Claudia's wedding (relatives of a PEZ executive) that took place October 6, 1978. They were used as place setting gifts and each guest received a set. The Bride is much harder to find than the Groom. It should be noted that the Bride's hair is different than the hair on the Nurse.

Orange Hair:	**$1700-$1900**
Brown Hair:	**$1800-$2000**
Blonde Hair:	**$1800-$2000**

Doctor and Nurse

Early 1970s, No Feet

Both of these dispensers are available in several versions. The doctor comes with OR without hair on either a blue, white, or yellow stem. The nurse can be found with brown, reddish orange, yellow, or blonde hair on several different stem colors. There is also a variation in her hat: one is a solid white and the other is an opaque or milky-white, semi-transparent color that is usually only found in dispensers that came from Canada.

Doctor:	**$150-$250**
Nurse:	**$150-$200**
Brazilian version Doctor (gray	
head band and stethoscope):	**$500+**
Brazilian version Nurse (black hair):	**$1000+**

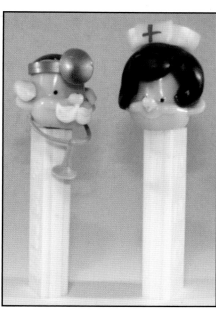

A rare pair: Brazilian variations of the Doctor and Nurse.

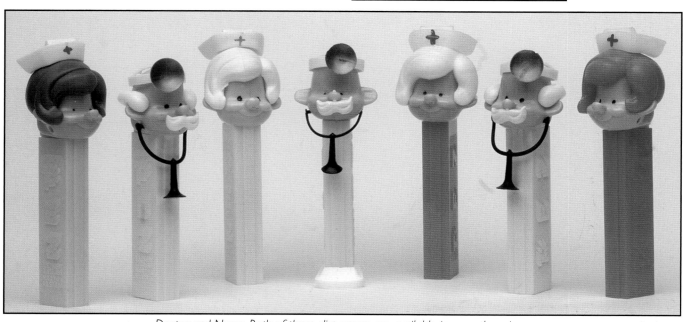

Doctor and Nurse. Both of these dispensers are available in several versions.

Engineer
Mid-1970s, No Feet
Value: $175-$200

Engineer from the mid-1970s.

Fireman
Early 1970s, No Feet
The Fireman was available with a dark moustache. White moustache rarities must be sealed in the package to be considered a variation. Notice the light gray badge variation on the Fireman on the far right.

Darker Badge:	$75-$90
Lighter Badge:	$150-$200
Brazilian version (black hat):	$1000+
Limited edition crystal head remake:	$25-$35

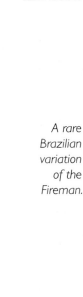

A rare Brazilian variation of the Fireman.

Fireman, from the early 1970s. Notice the one on the right has a slightly different color badge.

Girl
Early 1970s, No Feet and With Feet
The Girl can be found with either blonde or yellow hair.

No Feet:	$25-$35
With Feet:	$5-$10

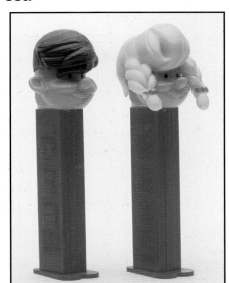

Boy and Girl or Valentine Boy and Girl. These are the most recent versions (no hole in nose).

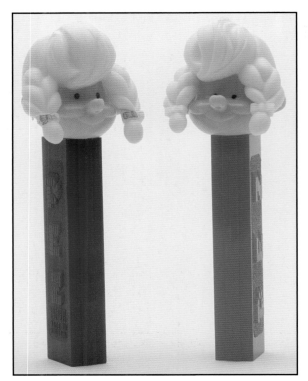

Girl, from the early 1970s. She can be found with blonde or yellow hair.

Groom

Late 1970s, No Feet

A rare dispenser from the October 6, 1978 wedding of Robert and Claudia (relatives of a PEZ executive).

Value: $500-$700

LIMITED EDITION Bride and Groom

Current, With Feet

New limited edition Bride and Groom dispensers (mail-order only).

Value: $30-$45 per set

Ethnic version: $30-$45 per set

Groom, a hard to find dispenser.

Limited Edition Bride and Groom (mail order only).

Ethnic version of the bride and groom (mail order offer from PEZ).

Knight

Early 1970s, No Feet

The Knight was available in three colors—red, black, or white. The white knight is the hardest to find. The plume color on the helmet must always match the stem in order to be correct.

Red: $400-$450

Black: $400-$500

White: $600-$700

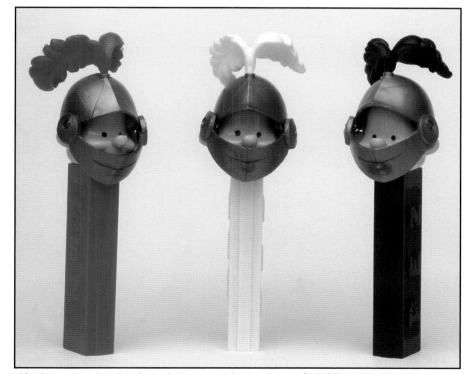

Knights—the white knight in the center is the hardest to find, followed by black then red.

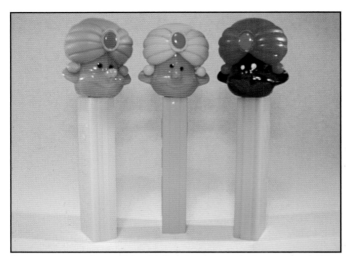

Some rare variations of the Maharaja, the version center and right are especially hard to find.

A selection of unusual Maharajas, the two on the left are from Spain.

Maharajah

Early 1970s, No Feet

There are several variations to this dispenser. One version, made in Hong Kong, has a slightly different turban than the others. Rare color turbans such as yellow or red are extremely rare and command high prices.

Hong Kong Version:	**$75-$85**
Darker Green Turban:	**$80-$100**
Lighter Green Turban:	**$60-$80**
Red or Yellow Turban:	**$2000+**
Spain version:	**$200-$300**

Maharajah, from the early 1970s. Notice the one on the far left. His turban is shaped slightly different than the other two. This is the "Hong Kong" version; the one in the middle has a darker green turban and the one on the right is the most common of the three.

Mexican

Mid-1960s, No Feet

With removable hat, goatee and earrings, this one can be tough to find with all of his pieces.

Value: **$200-$250**

A rare black variation.

Mexican, from the mid-1960s. This one can be tough to find with all of his pieces.

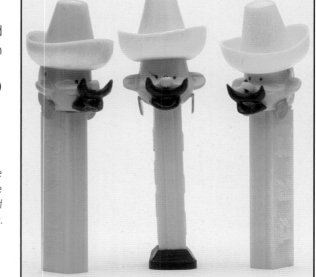

1990s PEZ Pals

Mid-1990s, With Feet

PEZ introduced a new PEZ Pals series in the mid-1990s designed specifically to be used with "Body Parts." Included in the series are a Pilot, Mariner, Shell Gas Attendant, Aral boy, and Alpine Boy. The series was not sold in the U.S. The pilot can be found with a white or blue hat and white or blue body parts. The white hat, white body part version is harder to find.

Value: **$8-$12 each**
With matching body partsoutfits: **$10-$15 each**
Glowing Head versions: **$5-$10**

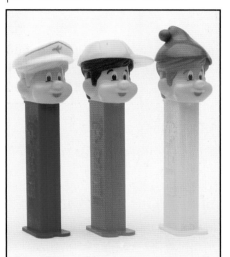

New PEZ Pal series from the mid-1990s. Left to right: Pilot, Shell Gas attendant, and Alpine boy.

New PEZ Pals glowing head versions.

They actually glow in the dark!

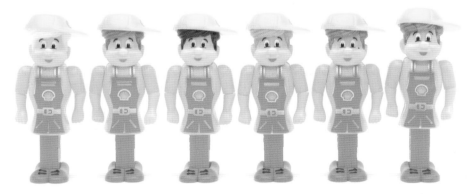

Shell PEZ Pals with hair color variations. White, Brown, Black, Gray, Silver, and Gold. Black hair is the most common.

Aral PEZ Pal with hair color variations. (Aral is a gas station in Europe.) Black hair is the most common followed by red then yellow.

New PEZ Pals in their matching Body Parts outfits.

Marineer and BP PEZ Pals in matching Body Parts.

Pirate

Early 1970s, No Feet

Variations can be found in the Pirate's bandana and in his skin tone.

Value: **$60-$85**

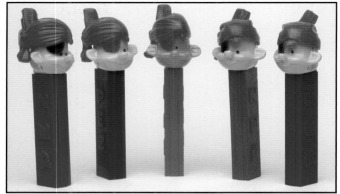

Pirates, from the early 1970s. There are three different variations shown here. The two on the left have a different scarf or bandanna than the two on the right. The dispenser in the middle has a flesh tone color variation that is very difficult to find.

Policeman

Early 1970s, No Feet

Value:	**$50-$75**
Limited edition crystal head remake:	**$25-$35**

Policeman, from the early 1970s.

Ringmaster

Mid-1970s, No Feet

An uncommon dispenser that is usually found missing his moustache.

Value: **$400-$450**

Limited edition crystal head remakes of the classic PEZ Pal.

Ringmaster, from the mid-1970s. It is common to find this dispenser missing his mustache.

Sailor

Late 1960s, No Feet
Value: **$150-$200**

Sailor, from the late 1960s.

Sheik

Early 1970s, No Feet
The Sheik can be found with either a red or black band on top of the burnoose.
Red Band: **$80-$100**
Black Band: **$100-$150**

Sheik, from the early 1970s.

Black band variation of the Sheik.

Sheriff

Late 1970s, No Feet
Value: **$150-$200**

Sheriff, from the late 1970s.

A selection of unusual PEZ Pals from Spain.

The First Regular!

Here it is, the original PEZ regular! This little guy is just over 3/4-inch wide and barely measures 2-1/2 inches tall. It matches the size of the mechanical drawing for patent number 2,620,061 exactly!

The original PEZ regular. Currently the only one in the world known to exist, it was found in a trash can!

The opposite side.

With the sleeve extended.

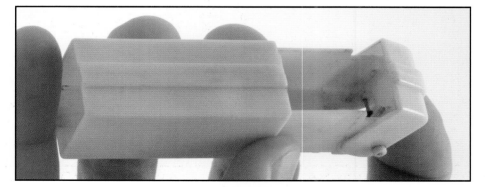

Advertising Regulars or Ad Regulars

These dispensers were never mass-produced. Most were screened one at a time and in very small quantities. They were given to customers and sales reps as "business cards." Ad Regulars are difficult to find, and from time to time previously unknown ads turn up. "Pez Haas" seems to be the most common, but others such as the NCWA convention or Walgreen's ad regulars are nearly impossible to find. The ultra-rare "Lonicot" regular is among the rarest of the advertising dispensers—only two are currently known to exist. Lonicot is German for "low nicotine." In the beginning, PEZ was touted as an alternative to smoking, so for a brief time they experimented with a candy that actually contained nicotine. This is the container that was to dispense that candy. To this date no candy has been found, only the dispenser and a small bit of paperwork.

Value: $2000-$3000 each
Lonicot Dispenser: $3000+
More Common Ads (Pez Haas Co.): $500-$1000 each

Bosch ad regulars.

A pair of rare ad regulars—in addition to the printing on the side, notice the writing on the front of the green dispenser.

A hard to find ad regular.

Another hard to find ad regular.

Advertising Regulars or Ad Regulars. These were never mass-produced.

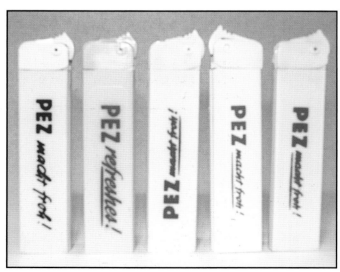

A selection of Macht-Froh ad regulars.

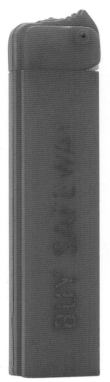

Safeway ad regular.   _The ultra-rare "Lonicot" regular._

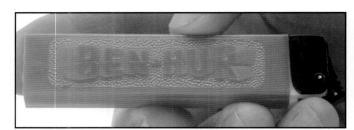

Ben Hur ad regular, currently one of two known.

A selection of hard to find ad regulars.

A selection of rare advertising regulars.

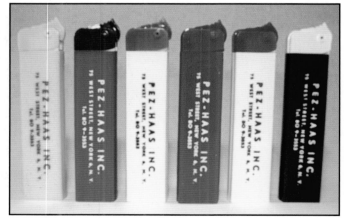

A selection of hard to find ad regulars.

A selection of hard to find ad regulars.

A selection of hard to find ad regulars.

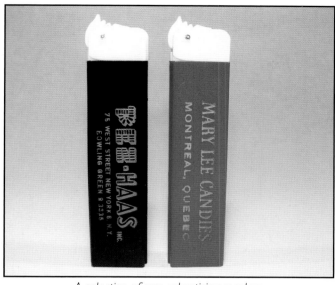

A selection of rare advertising regulars.

The stands these regulars are in are very difficult to find.

A selection of rare advertising regulars.

A selection of rare advertising regulars.

Front view of unusual printing found on a group of ad regulars.

Back view of the same group.

Another rare advertising regular is from Landis Ford.

Side view of the "Golden" PEZ dispenser.

Vivil is a direct competitor of PEZ in Europe and has been around since the early 1900s. These are not PEZ dispensers but something similar that was created to dispense Vivil tablets. As you can see, the size and shape of the candy was directly influenced by the PEZ design.

Arithmetic Dispensers

Early 1960s

Arithmetic Regulars were available as a mail-in premium as well as sold in stores. They can be found in red, blue, green, tan, and yellow.

Blue:	**$500-$700**
Green:	**$600-$800**
Red:	**$700-$900**
Tan or Yellow:	**$800-$1000**

Arithmetic dispensers were offered as a mail-in premium as well as sold in stores. Shown here with the original insert.

"Golden" regular as compared with a vintage regular. The Golden regular is slightly wider and deeper than a normal regular. Notice the Golden regular has a different style cap then the regular version. There are no markings or patent numbers on this dispenser other than the raised Golden script. Because of the size difference this is probably not a true PEZ dispenser, and it could have been made by the same company that produced the other bootleg dispensers years ago.

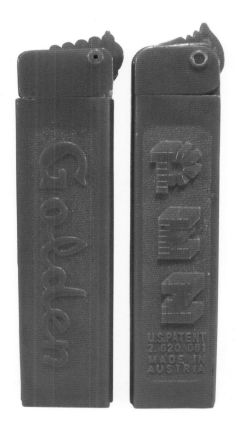

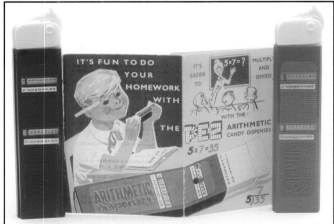

A variety of Arithmetic dispensers.

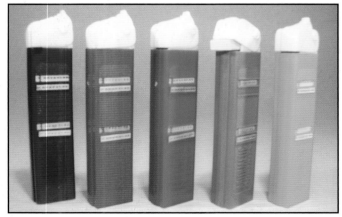

A selection of Arithmetic dispensers—they actually do math!

BOX trademark regular.

Box Trademark Regular

Late 1940s to early 1950s
Thought to be the first generation of dispenser design.

Value: $900-$1500

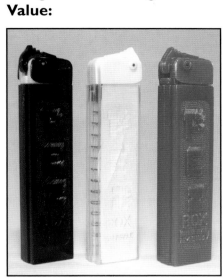

A selection of rare Box Trademark variations.

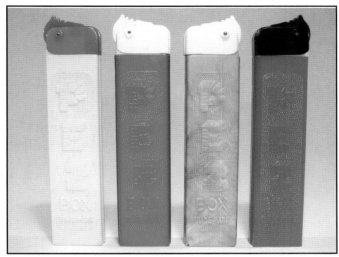

A selection of rare Box Trademark variations.

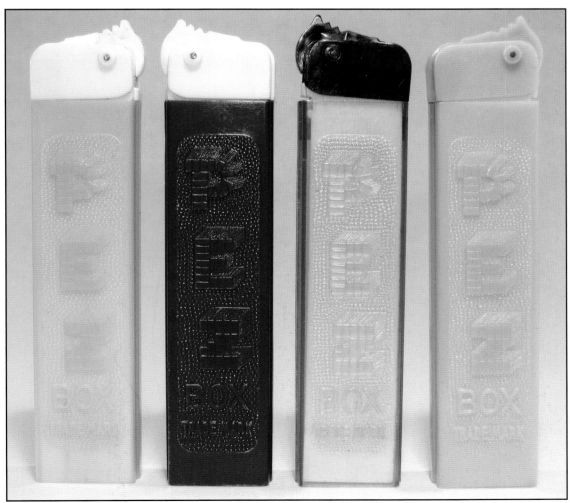

A selection of rare Box Trademark variations.

Box Patent Regular

Early 1950s

This is believed to be the second-generation dispenser design, the box trademark being the first. It was not sold in the U.S. and is a very rare dispenser.

Value: $900-$1200

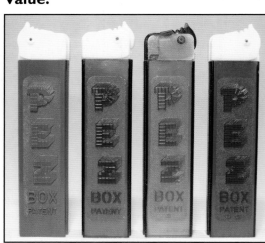

Box Patent regular (non-U.S.). A very rare dispenser.

A selection of blue Box Patents.

A selection of red Box Patents.

A selection of rare Box Patents.

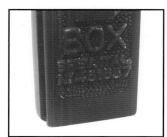

Detail of a VERY rare Italian Box Patent.

Locking Cap Regular (Trademark)

Late 1940s

Value: $4000+

A selection of rare Box Patents.

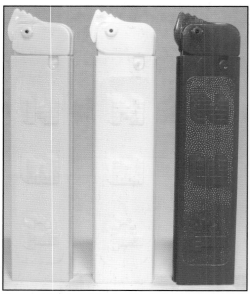

Three variations of the Locking Cap Regular, these are very difficult to find.

Rare Locking Cap Regular.

Golden Glow

This dispenser was offered only as a mail-in premium and is tough to find with finish in good condition—tarnish spots are common.

Value: $85-$125

Original Golden Glow still in the package!

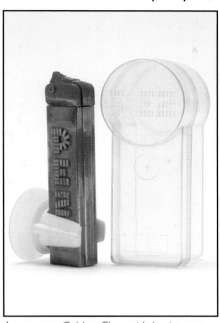

A very rare Golden Glow with Lucite case and suction cup holder.

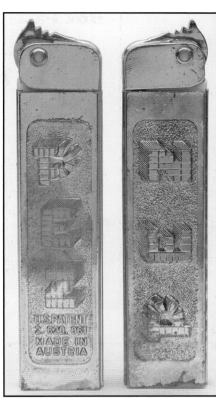

The Golden Glow dispenser was only offered through a mail-in promotion.

Newer Golden Glow regulars.

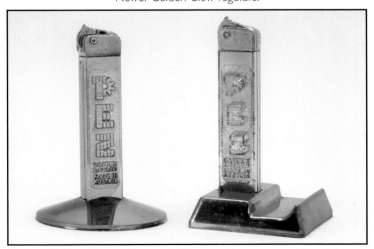

Vintage Golden Glows with stands. The round base is the older of the two.

New Golden Glow 50th anniversary dispenser! 2002 marked the 50th year of PEZ in America. To celebrate the milestone, PEZ re-created this vintage dispenser. One side of the cap is embossed 1952 the other 2002. Sold through a mail-order offer for the special price of $19.52!

New Regulars

Mid-1990s

A new line of Regulars were produced in the 1990s, but with a noticeable difference in the cap. There is also a new line of Regulars with different colors that are only available in Japan.

New U.S. Regulars:	**$3-$5**
Mono (sleeve is same color as cap and stem):	**$20-$25**
Japanese Regulars Pink, White, or Gray:	**$5-$10**
Japanese Black:	**$15-$20**
Japanese Gold:	**$30-$40**
Retro Regulars (set of 6 mail-order offer):	**$15-$20**

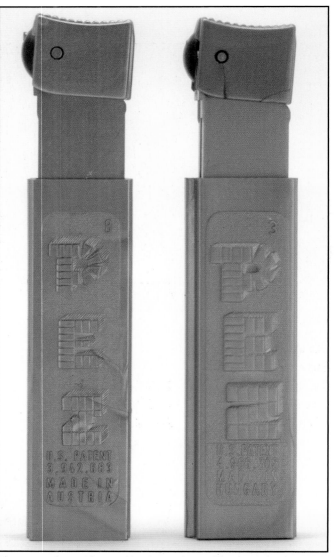

Rare long gray regular and "Klik and Spend" ad regular. These date to the early '70s.

Comparison of a new regular (on the left), and a vintage regular (on the right).

Newer regulars with matching inner sleeves. These are known as "mono regulars."

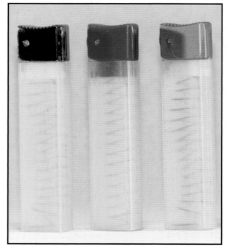

Unusual selection of "test" regulars.

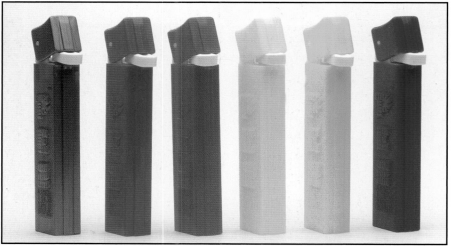

U.S. regular re-makes. First issued in the mid-1990s, mono toned (inner sleeve matches cap and stem) versions are tough to find and can sell for $20-$30 each.

Retro regulars offered through the PEZ mail-order program.

Regular re-makes found only in Japan in the mid 1990s. Gold is the most difficult to find followed by black. The other three seem to be more common.

Silver Glow
Early 1990s

Carded:	**$25-$40**
Loose:	**$15-$20**
80th Anniversary:	**$40-$50**

Special Silver Glow released to celebrate the 80th anniversary of PEZ.

Silver Glow, these were produced in 1991 to commemorate the opening of a new PEZ plant in Hungary.

Silver Glow, from the early 1990s.

Vintage Regulars
1950s

There are many different cap/stem color combinations including some that are semi-transparent through which you can see the inner workings of the dispenser.

Value: **$100-$150**

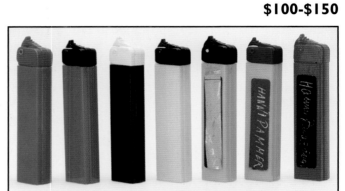

More vintage regulars with "personalized" variations.

WOW! A complete box full of vintage regulars! (Note: the early style twist tops on the cello bags.)

A collection of disposable regulars. These dispensers have blank sides, came pre-filled with candy, and once emptied, could not be refilled.

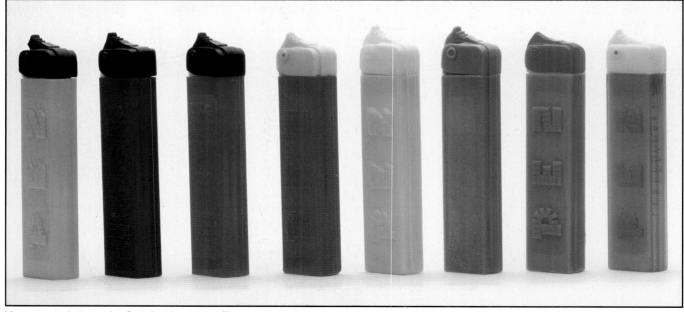

Vintage regulars can be found with many different cap and stem color combinations. The green dispenser on the far right is known as a "semi-transparent" because you can see the inner workings through the stem.

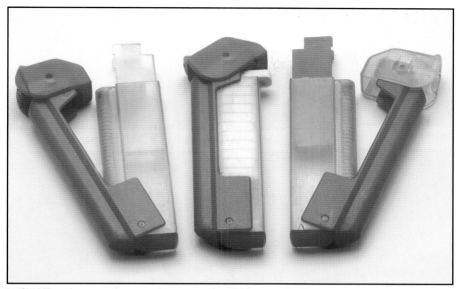

WOW! The ultra rare dispenser known as the "folding regular" or "super regular." They never went into production and few are known to exist. One sold on eBay in 2002 for $4500!

Vintage regular on card. Translation on card—"Fill me with PEZ and play with me."

A selection of vintage regulars.

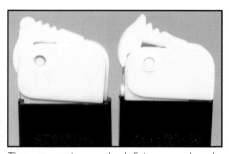

The cap version on the left is unusual and can be difficult to find.

A selection of blue vintage regulars.

A rare, clear plastic vintage regular.

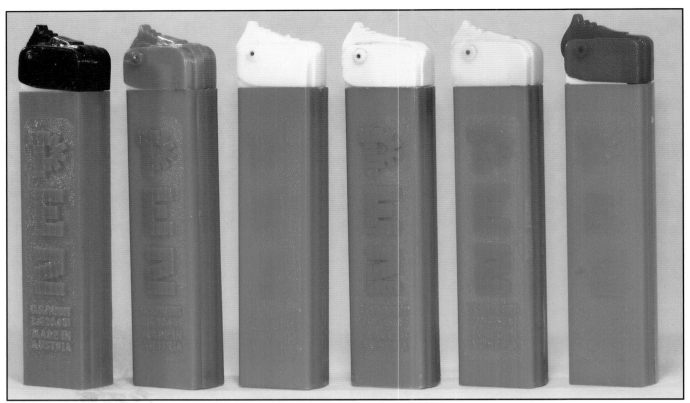

A selection of green vintage regulars.

A selection of vintage regulars.

A selection of red vintage regulars.

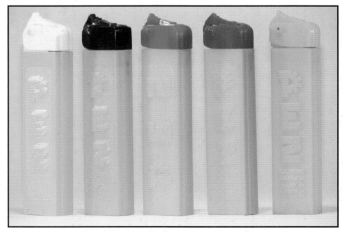

A selection of yellow vintage regulars.

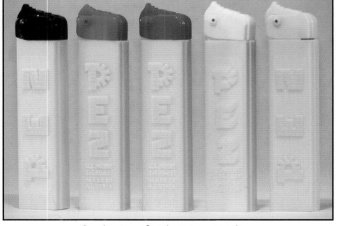

A selection of pink vintage regulars.

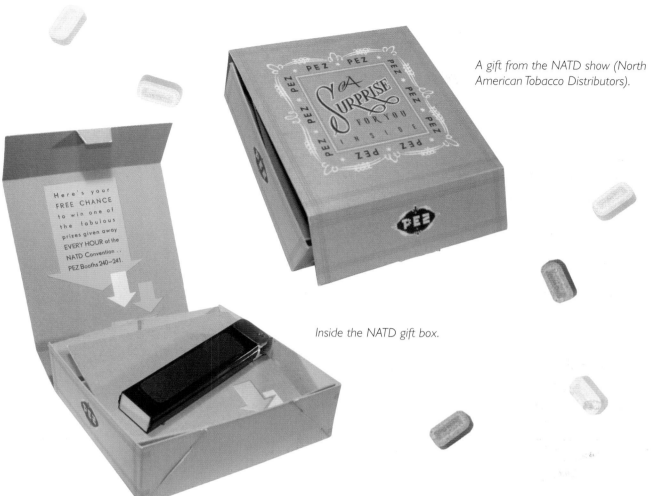

A gift from the NATD show (North American Tobacco Distributors).

Here's your FREE CHANCE to win one of the fabulous prizes given away EVERY HOUR at the NATD Convention . . . PEZ Booths 240–241.

Inside the NATD gift box.

Rare "Super Mint" card with regular.

Personalized Regulars

1950s

These regulars have one smooth side with a special sticker that allowed the owner to scratch his or her name on the side or "personalize" their dispenser. Pristine examples are difficult to find as most had some type of customization done to the side.

Value: **$150-$225**

A selection of personalized regulars.

A selection of vintage personalized regulars.

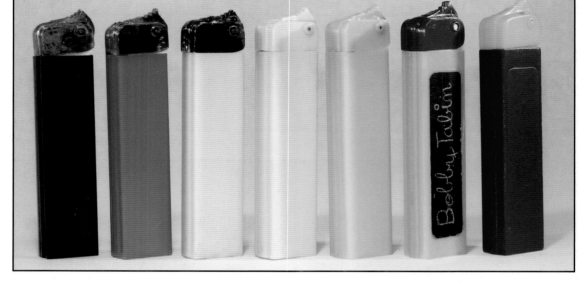

Transparent and U.S. Zone Regulars

1950s

Value: **$200-$250**

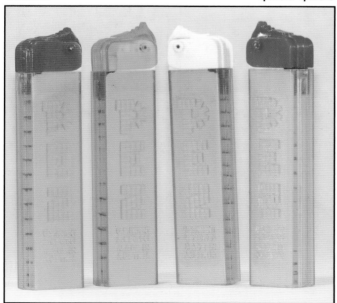

A selection of transparent yellow regulars.

A selection of transparent blue regulars.

A selection of U.S. Zone regulars.

Stem detail of a U.S. Zone regular.

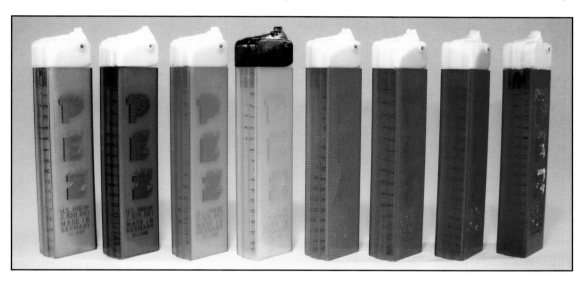

A selection of transparent U.S. Zone regulars.

Witch Regular
Mid-1950s

This is among the rarest of PEZ dispensers. A picture of a witch is screened on both sides of the stem.

Value: **$2500+**

Witch regulars. Light and dark orange variations. The same picture of the Witch is screened on both side of the stem.

CHAPTER 13

Superheroes

Batman

Late 1960s, No Feet and With Feet

Batman has gone through several different looks and can still be found today. Batman with Cape is the earliest version and collectors should be aware that reproductions of the cape have been made. The original cape is somewhat translucent whereas reproduction capes are much thicker.

Batman with Cape:	**$95-$120**
Short Ears, No Feet:	**$20-$30**
Short Ears, With Feet:	**$10-$15**
Short Ears, With Feet, Black	
(available for a very short time	
in the mid-1990s):	**$5-$10**
Pointy Ear Dark Knight:	**$2-$3**
Rounded Ear Dark Knight (Current):	**$1-$2**

Batman, first appeared in the late 1960s and is still produced today.(L to R): original, with feet, black (available for a very short time in the mid-1990s), pointy ear version of the Dark Knight, and round ear Dark Knight version.

Captain America

Late 1970s, No Feet

Captain America was produced with a black and a blue mask—the black mask is tougher to find.

Black Mask:	**$125-$150**
Blue Mask:	**$95-$120**

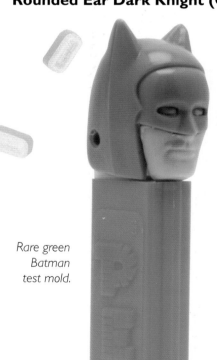

Rare green Batman test mold.

A selection of Batman variations.

Batman with Cape, from the late 1960s.

Captain America, black-mask version on left; blue-mask version on right.

Green Hornet

Late 1960s, No Feet

The Green Hornet was produced in two different versions—one with a small hat and the other with a larger hat. Hard to find variations can be found in either brown or gray and can sell for twice the price of a green hat version. The brown and gray hats are thought to be the early versions first released to the public. It is rumored the original photos submitted to create and model the character were in black and white. Not knowing the Green Hornet was supposed to have a green hat in addition to his green mask, they took the liberty of making the hat a more common brown or gray color. Once the mistake was realized the color quickly changed to green for all subsequent hats.

Version A (smaller hat):	**$200-$225**
Version B (larger hat):	**$175-$200**
Brown or Gray Hat:	**$400-$500**

Close-up of the Green Hornet head.

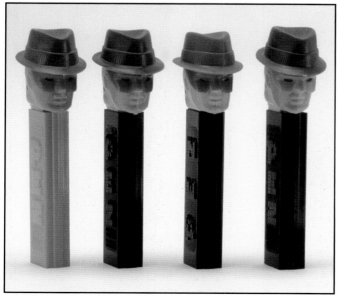

Green Hornet variations.

Green Hornet Version A with smaller hat.

Green Hornet Version B with larger hat.

Incredible Hulk. (L to R): Dark green, light green, light green with feet.

Incredible Hulk

Late 1970s, No Feet and With Feet

The Incredible Hulk dispenser has been produced in varying shades of green.

Dark Green, No Feet:	**$40-$50**
Light Green, No Feet:	**$45-$55**
Light Green, With Feet:	**$3-$5**
With Teeth (current version, released 1999):	**$1-$2**

One of a kind writing on the bottom sleeve of the white eyed Hulk, "endgultiges Muster E 19.5.78." Translation: "Final Sample May 19 1978."

Another version of the Incredible Hulk released in 1999.

Rare, white eye version of the Incredible Hulk.

Softhead Superheroes

Late 1970s, No Feet

The heads on these dispensers are made of a soft eraser-like material and usually found only on stems marked "Made in the USA." These are very popular with collectors. Characters in the series include: Batman, Penguin, Wonder Woman, Joker, and Batgirl.

Value: **$150-$200 each**

Softhead Superheroes. (L to R): Batman, Penguin, Wonder Woman, Joker, and Batgirl.

Spider-Man

Late 1970s, No Feet and With Feet
Several versions of Spider-Man have been produced over the years.

Smaller Head, No Feet:	**$15-$20**
Small Head, No Web Lines on Back of Head:	**$200+**
Medium Size Head, With Feet:	**$3-$5**
Larger Head, With Feet (Current):	**$1-$2**

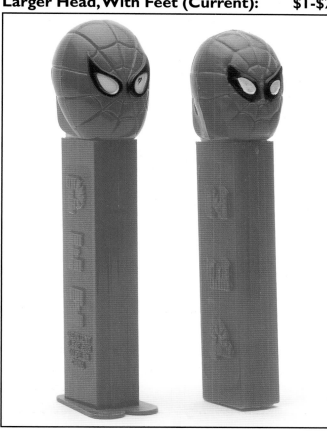

Spider-Man, first appeared in the late 1970s.

2000 Spider-Man. This version has a much bigger head than previous examples and is featured on a plain but unique card found only in Australia. $1-$3.

Copyright comparision; the version on the right has the copyright notice, the version on the left does not.

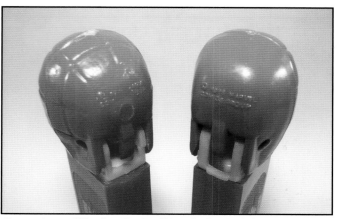

Comparision of "line" vs. "no line" heads. On the left version the lines come around the back of the head, on the right version they do not. The "no lines" version is much harder to find.

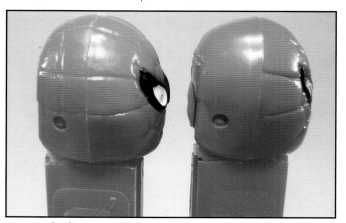

Profile comparisons of the line/no lines variations.

Thor

Late 1970s, No Feet
Value: **$300-$350**

Thor, from the late 1970s.

Wolverine

1999, With Feet
This is one of the characters from the popular X-Men comic.
Value: **$1-$2**

Wolverine, from the X-Men comic.

Wonder Woman

Late 1970s, No Feet and With Feet

Two versions of Wonder Woman were produced—the earlier has a raised star on her headband while on the second version the star is flat.

Raised Star,
No Feet: **$20-$25**
Raised Star,
** With Feet:**   **$5-$10**
Flat Star, With
** Feet (Current):**   **$1-$2**

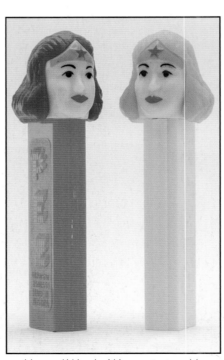

Unusual Wonder Woman test molds.

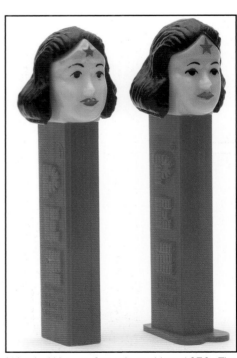

Wonder Woman, first released late 1970s. The dispenser on the left is the raised star version.

CHAPTER 14

Trucks

A Series Truck

Late 1960s

The A Series Trucks have two sets of wheels that roll and a single fender over the back wheels. Unusual cab colors such as burgundy or blood red can almost double the value. Three different cab styles can be found; A1, A4, and A16.

Value:	**$50-$75**
Rare silver truck:	**$500+**

A rare and unusual A Series variation with blue wheels.

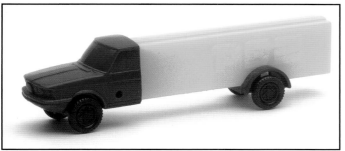

A Series truck.

Various A Series trucks.

A selection of A #1 trucks with brown cabs.

A selection of A #1 trucks.

A selection of A #1 trucks with green cabs.

A selection of A #16 trucks with blue cabs.

A selection of A #1 trucks.

A selection of A #16 trucks.

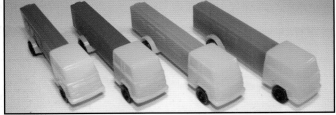

A selection of A #1 trucks with yellow cabs.

A selection of A #16 trucks.

A selection of A #4 trucks.

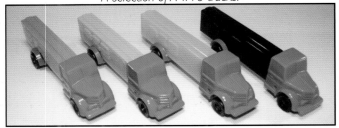

A selection of A #16 trucks with green cabs.

A selection of A #4 trucks with purple cabs.

A trio of A #4 mono trucks.

A selection of A #4 trucks with green cabs.

A selection of A #4 trucks.

B Series Truck

Late 1970s

The B Series Trucks have three sets of wheels that roll; one set in the front and two in the back. The wheels on a B Series are different than other truck wheels. It's not uncommon to find C Series wheels that have been incorrectly placed on a B Series truck. These wheels will not always roll as freely as they are supposed to and the shape of the wheel is incorrect. The fender on a B Series truck has a dip between the rear set of wheels. When standing the truck vertical, the back fender will resemble the capital letter B. There are three different cab styles in the B Series: B8, B9, and B13. There are some rare trucks that are marked BR1, BR2, BR3, and BR4—many of these were made in Brazil and are quite difficult to find.

Value:	**$40-$65**
Army Green (unusual color):	**$200-$250**
BR Series:	**$350+**

B Series truck.

B Series truck in rare olive green.

Various B Series trucks.

An army green trio of B Series trucks.

A selection of B #8 trucks with purple cabs.

A selection of B Series truck variations.

A selection of B #8 trucks with orange cabs.

A selection of B #13 trucks with blue cabs.

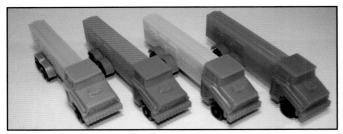

A selection of B #9 trucks with green cabs.

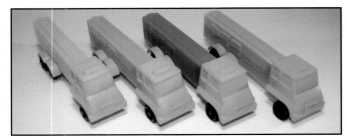

A selection of B #13 trucks with orange cabs.

A selection of B #9 trucks with blue cabs.

A selection of B #13 trucks with purple cabs.

Stem detail of a Brazil made truck.

Rare Brazil made trucks. Notice the wheels and fenders are positioned closer to the cab than other B Series trucks.

Rare blue B Series wheel on the left.

Rare white B Series wheel on the left.

A box full of vintage trucks!

C Series truck.

A selection of C #1 truck variations.

C Series Truck

Early 1980s

The C Series Trucks have three sets of wheels; one set in the front and two sets in the back that roll and a smooth fender over the rear set of wheels. Wheels on a C Series truck are similar in style to an A Series wheel but the C Series has a deeper "dish" than the A version. Several cab styles were used on these trucks; C1, C2, C3, C4, C5, and C16. Rare variations include dark blue and white wheel versions.

Value:	**$15-$25**
Blue Wheels:	**$200+**
White Wheels:	**$400+**

A selection of C #1 trucks with yellow cabs.

A selection of C #1 trucks with orange cabs.

A selection of C #1 trucks with blue cabs.

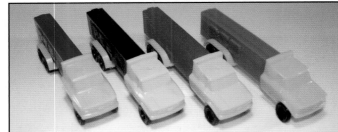

A selection of C #2 trucks with yellow cabs.

A selection of C #1 trucks variations.

A selection of C #2 trucks variations.

Various cab styles of the C Series truck.

A selection of C #2 trucks with blue cabs.

A selection of C #4 trucks with blue cabs.

A selection of C #2 truck variations.

A selection of C #4 truck variations.

A selection of C #3 truck variations.

A selection of C #4 truck variations.

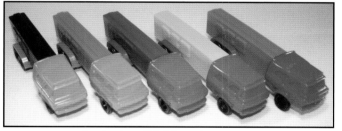

A selection of C #3 truck variations.

A selection of C #4 trucks with yellow cabs.

A selection of C #3 trucks with blue cabs.

A selection of C #5 trucks with blue cabs.

A selection of C #3 trucks with yellow cabs.

A selection of C #5 truck variations.

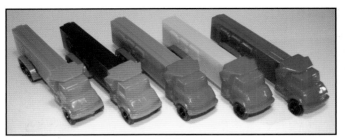

A selection of C #5 truck variations.

A selection of rare white wheel C Series trucks.

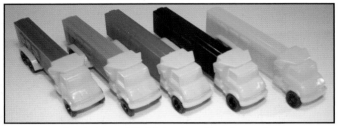

A selection of C #5 trucks with yellow cabs.

A selection of C #16 trucks with blue cabs.

A selection of rare white wheel C Series trucks.

A selection of C #16 trucks with red cabs.

A selection of rare white wheel C Series trucks.

A selection of C #16 truck variations.

A selection of rare white wheel C Series trucks.

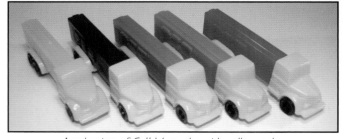

A selection of C #16 trucks with yellow cabs.

A selection of rare white wheel C Series trucks.

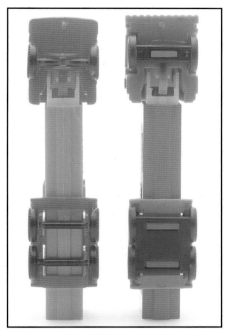

Comparison of the undersides of the C and D Series. The C Series (left) has moveable wheels; the wheels on the D Series (right) do not move.

Nivea truck is a promotional item from the Nivea Family Fest that was held in Austria 2003.

D Series Truck

Early 1990s-2000s

The D Series Trucks have six wheels and a smooth fender but, as of 1991, the wheels no longer move. Several cab styles can be found; R1, R2, R3, and R4.

Value:	**$2-$3**
Glow-in-the-Dark Version:	**$8-$12**
Blue Nivea Truck on card:	**$15-$20**

Various D Series test truck variations.

D Series trucks with glow-in-the-dark trailers.

D Series trucks.

A rare version of the Nivea truck.

E Series Rigs

2004

These trucks are the most realistic looking of any previous trucks and feature wheels that actually roll. There are four different cab styles and even a couple tanker trailer variations.

Value:	**$1-$2**
Cockta (Eastern European Soda):	**$40-$60**
NASCAR (2007):	**$2-$3**
Wal-Mart (2006):	**$2-$3**
Walgreens (2004):	**$2-$3**

Cockta is an Eastern European soda drink.

A selection of E Series trucks. The tanker versions are difficult to find.

A selection of E Series trucks.

Promotional item found only in Wal-Mart stores 2006.

Promotional item found only in Walgreens stores 2005.

NASCAR team trucks (L to R): Home Depot (Tony Stewart), Rusty's Last Call—Miller (Rusty Wallace), Dupont (Jeff Gordon), Dodge (Kasey Kahne), Dewalt (Matt Kenseth), and STP (Richard Petty).

NASCAR Hauler. Top row (L to R): Dodge (Kasey Kahne), Dewalt (Matt Kenseth), Home Depot (Tony Stewart). Bottom row (L to R): STP (Richard Petty), Rusty's Last Call—Miller (Rusty Wallace), Dupont (Jeff Gordon).

Promotional Truck

Approximately 8 inches long, these were produced in very small quantity and given to European food chains in 2001-2002. A second truck was done in 2003.

Value: **$20-$25**

Promotional toy truck. "Nashen & Spielen." Translation: "Eat and Play."

European promotional truck done in 2003.

CHAPTER 15

Camel

No Feet and With Feet
The camel can be found with either
a brown or a tan head.

No Feet:	**$65-$85**
With Feet:	**$60-$80**

Clown

No Feet and With Feet

No Feet:	**$30-$40**
With Feet:	**$5-$10**

Dog

No Feet and With Feet

No Feet:	**$30-$40**
With Feet:	**$20-$30**

Donkey

No Feet and With Feet

No Feet:	**$15-$25**
With Feet:	**$5-$10**

Duck

No Feet and With Feet

No Feet:	**$35-$45**
With Feet:	**$30-$40**

Frog

No Feet and With Feet

No Feet:	**$50-$65**
With Feet:	**$45-$60**

Indian

With Feet

Value:	**$20-$25**

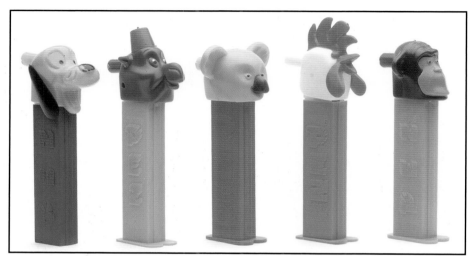

A group of Merry Music Makers. (L to R): Dog, Camel, Koala, Rooster, Monkey.

More Merry Music Makers. (L to R): Donkey, Tiger, Parrot, Rhino, Penguin.

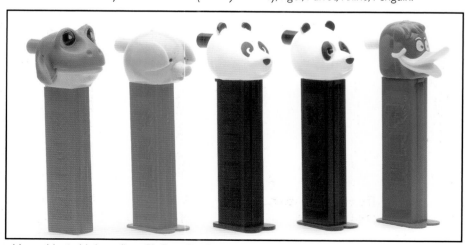

Merry Music Makers (L to R): Frog, Pig, Panda (stencil eyes), Panda (removable eyes), Duck.

The Whistles are also known as Merry Music Makers. PEZ began producing these musical dispensers in the early 1980s.

Koala
No Feet and With Feet
No Feet:	**$25-$35**
With Feet:	**$5-$10**

Lamb
No Feet and With Feet
No Feet:	**$20-$30**
With Feet:	**$15-$20**

Monkey
No Feet and With Feet
No Feet:	**$30-$40**
With Feet:	**$25-$30**

Owl
With Feet
The Owl is very rare and only a few are known to exist.
Value:	**$1500-$2000**

Clown whistle.   *Two views of the Indian whistle.*   *Lamb whistle.*

Panda
No Feet and With Feet
The Panda was made with removable eyes and with stencil eyes.
Removable Eyes, No Feet:	**$25-$35**
Removable Eyes, With Feet:	**$20-$25**
Stencil Eyes, With Feet:	**$5-$10**

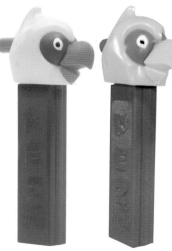

Owl whistle— this is a very rare dispenser.   *The two known variations of the rare Owl whistle.*   *Rare version of the Parrot whistle with red beak.*   *Rare yellow head Parrot whistle.*

Parrot
No Feet and With Feet
A rare variation of the Parrot exists with a yellow head and a red beak; more common versions have a red head with a yellow beak.
No Feet:	**$25-$35**
With Feet:	**$5-$10**
Yellow Head, Red Beak:	**$1000+**

Penguin
With Feet
Value:	**$5-$10**
Long Nose:	**$20-$30**

Pig
No Feet and With Feet
No Feet:	**$60-$80**
With Feet:	**$55-$75**
Black Head:	**$1000+**

Rhino
No Feet and With Feet
No Feet:	**$25-$35**
With Feet:	**$5-$10**

Rooster
No Feet and With Feet
No Feet:	**$25-$35**
With Feet:	**$20-$30**

Tiger
With Feet
Value:	**$5-$10**

Coach's Whistle
No Feet and With Feet
No Feet:	**$50-$75**
With Feet:	**$1-$3**

Some very rare color variation examples.

An assortment of the Coach's Whistle.

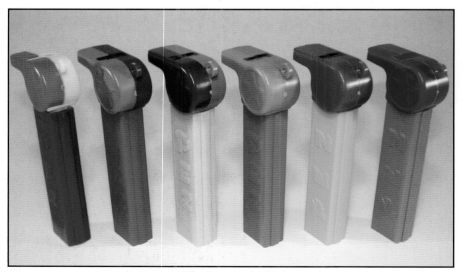

A selection of footless coach whistle variations.

A selection of footless coach whistle variations.

A selection of footless coach whistle variations.

A selection of footless coach whistle variations.

A selection of newer coach whistle variations.

In June 2000, the Chicago Cubs be-
came the first professional sports team to have a "PEZ dispenser day." The first 15,000 fans through the Wrigley Field gates received a limited edition Charlie Brown dispenser with a commemorative souvenir card. Other teams took notice of the Cubs' huge success and started their own "PEZ day" at the ball park. This trend is not limited to just major league baseball, teams such as the Orlando Magic and Washington Wizards (basketball) and Philadelphia Kixx (soccer) have followed suit.

With the wide variety of sports and sports teams, the possibilities are almost limitless. Initial offerings of these dispensers on Internet auction sites saw prices in the $50 range. Prices have since come down and seem to have leveled in the $20-$30 range. Most of these events gave away 15,000 dispensers, a **very** small quantity in relation to the number PEZ makes of a normal character dispenser sold at the retail level. Given the small number, and the fact these events are usually local or at best regional one-day events, I think these special dispensers will continue to hold a higher value, not only with PEZ collectors but with sports memorabilia collectors as well.

Dispensers and teams to date:

2000 June 14 - Cubs Charlie Brown with logo on cap: $15-$25
2001 June 26 - Cubs Joe Cool with logo on baseball cap: $15-$25
2001 July 8 - Minnesota Twins T.C. Bear: $10-$15
2001 September 15 - Chicago Cubs Homer Simpson with sticker on bag: $15-$25
2001 September 23 - Philadelphia Phillies baseball with team logo: $15-$25
2001 October 6 - Chicago Cubs Homer Simpson: $15-$25
2001 November 9 - Orlando Magic basketball with team logo: $20-$30
2002 February 3 - Washington Wizards basketball with team logo: $20-$30
2002 March 2 & 3 - Philadelphia Kixx white ball with team logo
(only 2500 were given out each day): $20-$30
2002 March 15 - New Jersey Nets basketball with team logo: $20-$30
2002 June 27 - Chicago Cubs baseball with team logo: $15-$25
2002 June 28 - Columbus Clippers baseball with team logo: $10-$15
2002 July 5 - New York Yankees baseball with team logo: $15-$25
2002 July 14 - Minnesota Twins baseball with team logo: $10-$15
2002 August 2 - Washington Mystics (WNBA) white basketball with team logo: $20-$30
2002 August 14 - Chicago Cubs Charlie Brown: $15-$25
2002 August 28 - Yankees (Staten Island) baseball: $15-$25
2002 September 14 - Arizona Diamondbacks baseball with team logo: $15-$20
2002 October 30 - Seattle Super Sonics Basketball: $20-$30
2003 April 21 - LSU Tigers baseball: $15-$20

2003 June 16 - Minnesota Twins T.C. Bear (2nd release): $10-$15
2003 July 21 - New York Yankees Charlie Brown: $15-$25
2004 - Sweden Soccer Team Soccer Ball: $20-$25
2004 Metro Stars (European Hockey Team) puck: $10-$15
2004 LSU Football: $20-$30
2005 July 30 - Connecticut Suns Basketball: $20-$30
2006 Florida State Football (carded): $3-$5
2006 Penn State Football (carded): $3-$5
2006 University of Alabama Football (carded): $3-$5

2006 University of Florida Football (carded): $3-$5
2006 University of Georgia Football (carded): $3-$5
2006 University of Michigan Football (carded): $3-$5
2006 University of Texas Football (carded): $3-$5
2006 Gold soccer ball with Italian flag: $3-$5
2007 Notre Dame Football (carded): $3-$5
2007 University of Louisville Football (carded): $3-$5
2007 Ohio State Football (carded): $3-$5
2007 Metro Stars (European Hockey team) DEG Lion: $15-$20

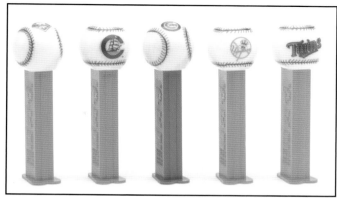

Chicago Cubs Joe Cool, Minnesota Twins T.C. Bear, Philadelphia Kixx soccer ball, Washington Wizards basketball, New Jersey Nets basketball .

Philadelphia Phillies, Columbus Clippers, Chicago Cubs, New York Yankees, Minnesota Twins.

Cubs Charlie Brown w/card: $15-$25.

Homer Simpson with commemorative card, $15-$25.

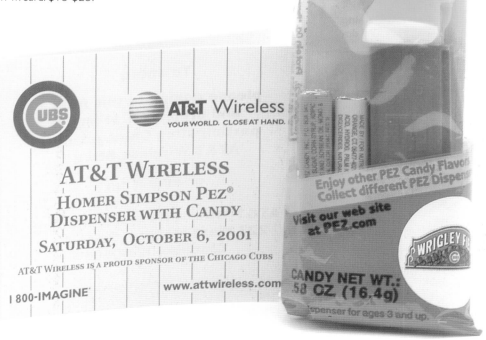

(L to R): Washington Mystics(2002), Seattle Super Sonics (2002), and Connecticut Suns (2005) basketballs.

(L to R): Arizona Diamondbacks (2002) and LSU Tigers(2003) baseballs.

Charlie Brown Cubs hat (2002) and Charlie Brown New York Yankees hat (2003).

Sweden SvFF Soccer team variations (2004).

Philadelphia Kixx soccer ball (2002).

Gold Italian soccer ball (2006).

S
P
O
R
T
S

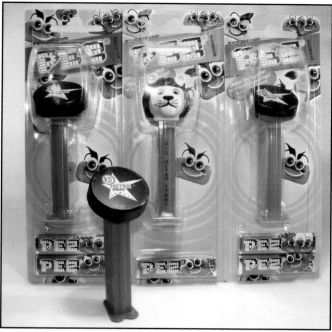

Metro stars (European hockey team) blue stem hockey puck, DEG Lion (team mascot) red stem hockey puck.

Notre Dame and Ohio State footballs.

This gold football was never sold at retail.

Baseball, football, basketball, and hockey puck were a PEZ mail order offer.

University of Alabama, Penn State, University of Michigan, and Florida State.

University of Florida, Louisianna State University, University of Texas, University of Georgia, and Tennessee (this one was never released).

CHAPTER 17

Miscellaneous Dispensers

Baseball Set

Mid 1960s, No Feet

This set consisted of a dispenser with a baseball mitt, removable ball, bat, and home plate. It is difficult to find with the bat and home plate. A box of 24, mint example vending boxes with their original contents was discovered in 2005. Until this point the vending boxes were nearly impossible to find. The "find" was quickly absorbed into the hobby and this set remains difficult to find with the original box.

**Glove and Ball
Only:**   **$150-$200**

**Glove, Ball, Bat
  and Home Plate: $400-$500**

With Vending Box: $600-$800

Baseball set, from the mid-1960s. This is difficult to find with the bat and home plate. The vending box is also very rare, only a few examples are known to have survived.

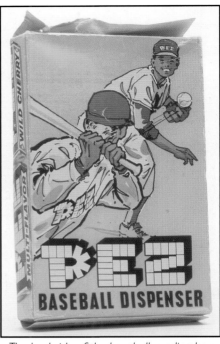

The backside of the baseball vending box.

Bear

Late 1990s, With Feet

This dispenser uses the same head as the Icee Bear and the FAO Schwarz Bear and is not available in the U.S.

Value: **$5-$10**

Boston Scientific

2004, With Feet

A promotional dispenser for a medical device company.

Value: **$25-$35**

Bears, from the late 1990s. These are unusual color variations.

Promotional dispenser done for Boston Scientific (a medical device company).

Back view of the Boston Scientific dispenser.

Breast Cancer Awareness

2004, With Feet

A special dispenser developed by a collector to raise money for the Susan G. Komen Foundation. All proceeds from the sale of this dispenser have been donated by this dealer for breast cancer research.

Value: **$10-$15**

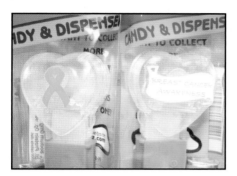

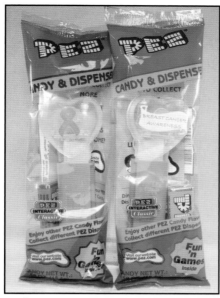

Breast cancer awareness dispensers.

Money raised from the sale of these dispensers is donated by a collector to the Susan G. Komen Foundation.

Bundesrat

2005, With Feet

The Bundesrat is one of the five permanent constitutional organs of the Federal Republic of Germany. These dispensers were given away with a safety game for children in 2005. For some reason the girl is easier to find than the boy.

Boy (loose):	**$15-$20**
Boy (carded):	**$20-$25**
Girl (loose):	**$10-$15**
Girl (carded):	**$15-$20**

Bundesrat dispensers, the carded versions are tough to find.

Bubbleman

Mid-1990s, With Feet

This dispenser was only available from PEZ through a mail-in offer. The Bubbleman was the first set offered in this manner. They have the copyright date of 1992 on the dispenser but didn't appear until the fall of 1996.

Original Bubbleman:	**$5-$10 each**
Neon Bubbleman (1998):	**$3-$6 each**
Crystal Bubbleman (1999):	**$3-$6 each**
Glowing Bubbleman:	**$3-$6 each**
Golden Bubbleman:	**$100+**

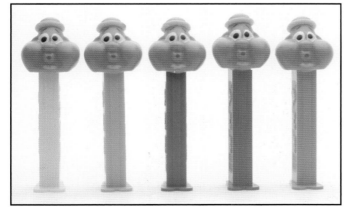

Bubbleman, only available from PEZ mail-in offer. This is the first set offered. They have the copyright date of 1992 on the dispenser, but didn't appear until the fall of 1996.

Neon Bubbleman, set of five available from PEZ mail-in offer. First appeared in 1998 with the matching neon color hat and stem.

Crystal Bubbleman, set of five available from PEZ mail-in offer. First appeared summer of 1999.

Golden Bubbleman.

Glow in the dark Bubbleman. Available through mail order offer only.

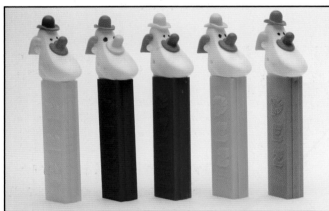

Clown with Chin (Also known as Long Face Clown)

Mid-1970s, No Feet

This dispenser can be found with many hair, hat, and nose color combinations.

Value: **$90-$120**

Long Face Clown or Clown with Chin, from the mid-1970s.

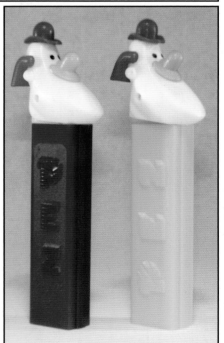

Clown with Collar

1960s, No Feet

Value: **$60-$75**
Yellow hat: **$300+**

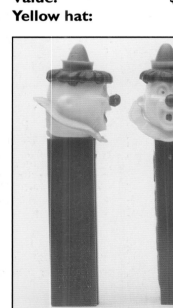

Long Face Clown variations.

Clown with Collar, from the 1960s.

The yellow hat version of Clown with Collar is quite rare.

Convention dispensers

2002 to current

These dispensers were done for the annual PEZ collector conventions. Each guest received one of these special edition dispensers with their registration packet. Initially, each of the dispensers created for the U.S. conventions were produced in colors that do not normally exist for that dispenser making them a "must have" for collectors.

2002 - Glow in the Dark Witch (USA):	**$15-$20**
2003 - Crystal Head Snowman (USA):	**$20-$25**
2003 - Linz Red Heart (European convention):	**$15-$20**
2003 - Pez-A-Go!Go! 7 (Japan):	**$25-$30**
2004 - Crystal Head Bee (USA):	**$20-$25**
2004 - Crystal Earth (European convention):	**$20-$25**
2004 - Pez-A- Go!Go! 8 LINK (Japan):	**$25-$30**
2005 - Chick in Egg (USA):	**$20-$25**
2005 - Crystal Hand (European convention):	**$20-$25**
2006 - No convention dispenser produced for the U.S. conventions	
2006 - Football (European convention):	**$20-$25**
2007 - A Regular Bugz Dispenser, only front of stem is printed (U.S.): $5-$10	

Convention dispenser from the first Linz gathering.

Convention dispensers from the Linz Gathering; earth (2004), hand & earth (2005), football (2006).

Convention dispensers: Witch (2002), Snowman (2003), Bee (2004), Chick (2005) and Bee (2007).

Convention dispenser Japanese Flag on Heart

2004, No Feet

Only 400 made for Japanese PEZ convention.

Value: **$20-$30**

Convention dispenser from Pez-A-GoGo 8 Aug. 21, 2004 in Tokyo, Japan.

Convention dispenser from Pez-A-GoGo 7 Nov. 23, 2003 in Tokyo, Japan.

Convention dispenser from one of the first Japanese conventions.

Crazy Fruit Series

Mid-1970s, No Feet

The Orange first appeared in the mid-1970s, followed by the Pear and Pineapple in the late 1970s. The Pineapple is the hardest of the three to find, followed by the Pear then the Orange. The Lemon was made as production sample but never produced.

Orange:	**$200-$250**
Pear:	**$600-$700**
Pineapple:	**$2500-$3000**
Lemon:	**$5000+**

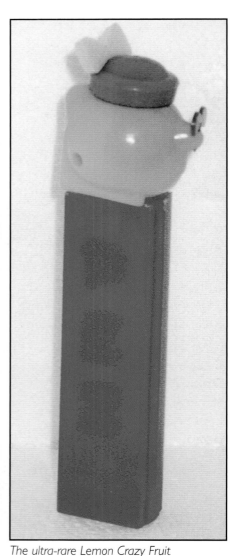

Crazy Fruit series with the Lemon.

The ultra-rare Lemon Crazy Fruit dispenser—this is a production sample; the dispenser was never produced.

Ultra-rare short stem pineapple on the left and regular version on the right. Notice the sticker on the stem, it says "Ananas-Hong/Kong.nicht/ genehmigte Aus/ fuhrung.26.6.78." Translation: "Pineapple Hong Kong not accepted variation 06-26-78."

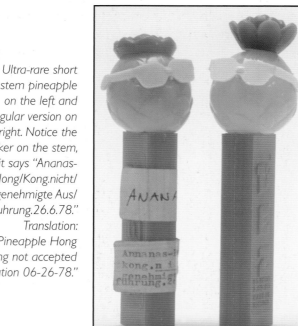

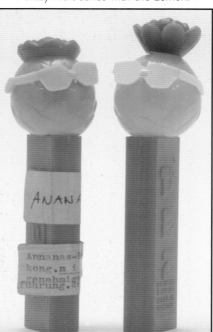

Crazy Fruit series. (L to R): Pear, Orange, and Pineapple.

Crystal Ball dispensers.

Crystal Ball Dispenser

Sold through a 2002 mail-in offer for $15.95. It has tiny silver sparkles in the stem and base. The first 2,500 were made by mistake using silver stars, the remaining production has blue stars.

Value:	**$15-$20**
Yellow Stars:	**$40-$50**

An hard to find yellow star variation of the Crystal Ball dispenser.

Die-Cuts

Early 1960s

A Die-Cut dispenser is one in which a design is cut into the side of the stem. The cut-out usually reveals an inner sleeve of a different color. Several dispensers were made with a die-cut stem in the 1960s.

Casper:	**$250-$275**
Donald Duck:	**$150-$175**
Mickey Mouse:	**$175-$225**
Easter Rabbit:	**$400-$550**
Bozo:	**$165-$200**

Die-cuts from the early 1960s. (L to R): Casper, Donald Duck, Mickey Mouse, Easter Rabbit, Bozo.

Earth

2003, No Feet

Special mail-order dispenser, this was to be the first in a "PEZ Planets" series but no other dispensers have been produced.

Value: $15-$20

Planet Earth was a mail-order offer from PEZ.

This special glow in the dark dispenser was only given to eBay employees.

eBay Dispensers

Available on-line from the eBay store in 2000, this set of four dispensers was sold for $10 per set. Limited to 5000 sets, they quickly sold out. eBay also presented their employees with a variation of this dispenser. It has a black base, glow in the dark heart with black eBay logo.

Crystal set of four:	**$40-$60**
Employee dispenser:	**$35-$65**

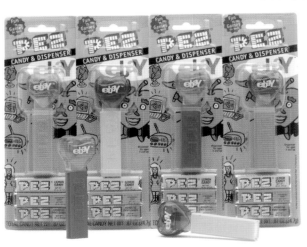

eBay hearts.

Emergency Heroes

2003, With Feet

This was a very popular series done to recognize some of America's hard working heroes.

Value: $1-$3

Black Fireman or Construction Worker: $5-$8

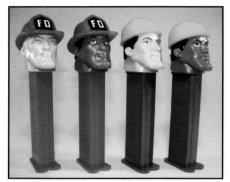

Policeman, K-9 dog, Policewoman.

Fireman and Construction workers.

Army soldier, Diver, Jet Pilot, and Nurse.

FAO Schwarz Bear

1999, With Feet

This dispenser was sold only in FAO Schwarz toy stores. This bear first appeared in late August of 1999 and had a retail price of $3.99.

Value: $5-$8

FAO Schwarz Bear—sold only in FAO Schwarz toy stores in 1999.

Funky Faces

2003, With Feet

Thirteen different expressions and many different stem colors make it fun to collect all of the variations.

Value: $1-$2

Funky Face (L to R): Kissy Face, Cheeky Eyelashes, Crying Face, and Baby Face.

Funky Face (L to R): Mischievous Smile, Angry Face, Embarrassed Face, and Smiley Tongue Face.

Funky Face (L to R): Open Smile, Sunglass Smile, Nerdy Face, Smiley Face, and Winking Smile.

Hard Rock Café

2006, With Feet

PEZ International hosted an after show party during the Cologne Candy Fair in Germany. They were done as a promotional give-a-way to those who attended the party and were produced in **very** small quantity.

Value: $100+

Promotional dispenser done for the Cologne Candy Fair 2006.

FX Toy Show – see Psychedelic Hands

Jack in the Box promotion, 2000. This is the same dispenser used in the 1999 promotion but now with a price of only 99 cents.

Jack in the Box

1999, With Feet

This is a restaurant promotion done in the likeness of the Jack in the Box mascot "Jack." It appeared for a very limited time in June of 1999 and was repeated briefly the following summer of 2000. Jack in the Box, found mostly in western states, allowed customers to buy these with an additional food purchase for $1.99. Three different stem colors: red, blue, and yellow.

Value: $3-$5

Foodmaker variation: $5-$10

Jack in the Box dispenser on 1999 promotional poster.

Jeffrey the Bunny (Dylan's Candy Bar)

2004, No Feet

Dylan's Candy Bar (owned by Ralph Lauren's daughter Dylan) has immortalized their famous chocolate bunny "Jeffrey" as a PEZ dispenser.

Value: $5-$8 on card

Loose: $4-$6

The chocolate bunny mascot of Dylan's Candy Bar stores.

Jungle Mission

Everything you will need the next time you're lost in the jungle! A flashlight, ruler, compass, backpack clip, magnifying glass, and most important—a PEZ dispenser! This can be found in several different color combinations.

Value: $2-$3 each

Jungle Mission Survival Kit.

Katrina

2005, With Feet

Requested by a collector and assisted by PEZ USA, 750 of these special dispensers were created as a fund raising effort to benefit victims of hurricane Katrina.

Value: $50-$60

1 of 750 dispensers created to raise funds for hurricane Katrina victims.

Magic PEZ dispenser

Dispenses candy from the hat and has an additional compartment on the bottom that holds an extra pack of candy that you can make disappear then magically re-appear! This can be found in many different color combinations.

Value: **$2-$3 each**

Magic PEZ dispenser.

Make-a-Face

Early 1970s, No Feet

This dispenser first appeared in 1972 but was quickly discontinued as it had too many tiny pieces that could be easily removed and swallowed by a child. Also, the dispenser was poorly packaged—the bubble frequently came loose from the card spilling the parts, rendering it unsellable. It is rumored what stock was left of these after they were discontinued was ground up, re-melted and used to mold the headdress for the Indian Chief. The U.S. version contained 17 separate pieces and the European 16, not counting the shoes. This is a very difficult dispenser to find still intact on the card.

U.S. version m.o.c.: **$3500+**
European version
m.o.c.: **$4000+**

Front of U.S. card.

Back of U.S. card.

A loose Make-a-Face dispenser.

Front of European card.

Back of European card.

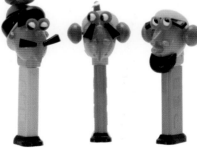

A trio of Make-a-Faces!

Mozart and Sissy

2007, With Feet

A special PEZ exhibit was held in Vienna to celebrate the 80th anniversary of the company. Two of Vienna's most famous residents were Mozart who is one of the world's most famous composers and Sissi, wife of Emperor Franz Joseph, also known as Empress Elisabeth. Since her reign in the late 1800s she has been known as "the little darling of Vienna."

Value: **$10-$15 each**

Two of Vienna Austria's most famous residents; Mozart and Empress Elisabeth (Sissi).

Special dispensers created for a candy exhibit in Vienna Austria honoring PEZ's 80th anniversary.

Mr. Mystic

1960s, No Feet

Some doubt the authenticity of this piece, citing it as nothing more than the head of Zorro with a ringmaster hat on it. This is incorrect, there is currently documentation from PEZ International that states his existence, and extensive research confirms this is a legitimate dispenser.

Value: **$500+**

The mysterious Mr. Mystic.

NASCAR Helmets

2005, With Feet

NASCAR has become the one of the biggest sporting branches of all time. Given its huge fan base and drivers' propensity to change teams, I think the potential value of these dispensers could rise significantly in the next few years. The original line up of seven divers included Jeff Gordon, Rusty Wallace, Matt Kenseth, Tony Stewart, Kasey Kahne, Bobby LaBonte, and Richard Petty. Dale Earnhardt Jr. and Jimmy Johnson dispensers debuted in 2007.

Value: **$1-$2**

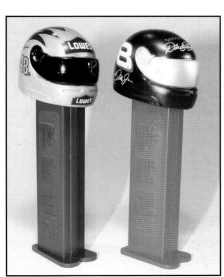

NASCAR helmets from 2007: #48 Jimmy Johnson and # 8 Dale Earnhardt Jr.

NASCAR helmets (L to R): #17 Matt Kenseth, #2 Rusty Wallace, #24 Jeff Gordon, #43 Richard Petty, #9 Kasey Kahne, #20 Tony Stewart, and #2 Bobby LaBonte.

Olympic Snowman

No Feet

This dispenser was made for the 1976 winter Olympics in Innsbruck, Austria. A very hard to find dispenser, it can also be found in a "short nose" version.

Value: **$500-$600**

Long-nose version of the Olympic Snowman from the 1976 Winter Olympics in Innsbruck, Austria.

A paper advertisement showing the Olympic Snowman valued at $50+.

Olympic Snowman still on the card!

A trio of rare black head Olympic Wolves.

Olympic Wolves (also called Vucko [voo sh-co] Wolves)

With Feet and No Feet

This hard to find dispenser was made for the 1984 Olympic games in Sarajevo, Yugoslavia. Lots of variations exist such as; hat, no hat, bobsled helmet, red nose, and gray nose versions. Light gray, dark gray, brown, and black head colors also exist. Gray nose and black head versions are the hardest to find.

Wolf, no hat:	**$175-$225**
Wolf, no hat, gray nose:	**$250-$300**
Wolf with hat:	**$250-$300**
Wolf with bobsled helmet:	**$250-$350**

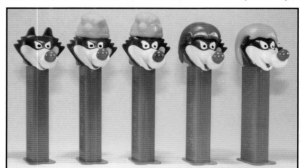

A selection of brown head Olympic Wolves with feet.

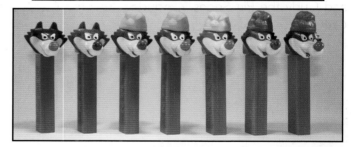

A selection of gray head Olympic Wolves.

A selection of gray head Olympic Wolves with feet.

A selection of Olympic Wolves with bobsled helmets. The marbleized and blue helmets are especially rare.

Vucko, the Olympic Wolf from the 1984 Sarajevo Olympics. Shown here with a paper insert.

Vucko variations; without hat, with hat, and with bobsled helmet.

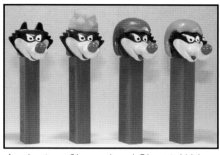

Both the Olympic symbol and Olympic rings appear on the back of Vucko's head.

A selection of brown head Olympic Wolves.

PEZ Petz
1998

Series 1 includes Zippy the dog, Grinz, the Monkey, Butler the Penguin, and Curly the Pig. Series 2 includes Purrl the Cat, Sidney the Kangaroo, Cheeky the Monkey, and Blubbers the Whale. Different than a traditional PEZ dispenser, these little characters have a sliding door that you slide back to dispense a piece of square gum.
Value: $1-$3

PIF the Dog
With Feet and No Feet

PIF was offered as a premium in a German "YPS" comic in 1989. If you look closely you can see his name PIF on his left ear.
Value: $100-$120

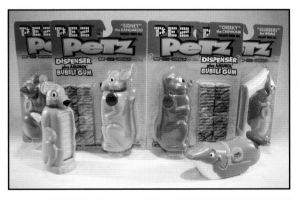

PEZ Petz (L to R): Purrl the Cat, Sidney the Kangaroo, Cheeky the Monkey, and Blubbers the Whale.

PEZ Petz (L to R): Zippy the dog, Grinz the Monkey, Butler the Penguin, and Curly the Pig.

PIF the Dog—a German comic character.

175

Playworld Sets

Early 1990s, With Feet, Non-U.S.

These sets featured a single dispenser along with a matching body part. The sets usually have a theme such as Easter or Christmas. After opening the package, the cardboard piece inserted with it would unfold into three sections. It contained related scenery that could serve as a backdrop to play with the dispenser.

Easter set:	**$20-$25**
Christmas set:	**$5-$10**
Shell Gas set:	**$20-$25**

Easter Playworld set.

Shell Gas Playworld set.

Christmas Playworld set.

Plush

Cuddle Cubs

2006

Valentine's Day plush dispenser with key chain.

Value: $2-$4

Cuddle Cub "Love" bears.

Fuzzy Friend Cats.

Fuzzy Friend Dogs.

Barnyard Babies

2005

Easter plush dispensers with key chain.

Value: $2-$4

Plush Barnyard Babies (L to R): Pig, Ducky, Lamb, Donkey, and Cow.

Fuzzy Friends

First released in 2000 each bear has a name, birth date, and hometown. Each bear has "PEZ" embroidered down the side of the stem, a backpack clip, and articulated arms and legs. A new series released in 2002 called "Wild Zoo" has five similar animal dispensers.

Fuzzy Friends Bears:	$2-$3 each
Fuzzy Friend Cats:	$2-$3 each
Fuzzy Friends Dogs:	$2-$3 each
Wild Zoo:	$3-$4 each

Fuzzy Friends (L to R): Purple bear is Gilbert, Black and White bear is Jade, Orange bear is T.J., and the Brown bear is Buddy.

Party Animals

2007

Republican Elephant or Democratic Donkey with key chain.

Value: $3-$4

Donkey and Elephant to commemorate the Democratic and Republican political parties.

Safari Animals

2005

Plush jungle animals with key chain.

Value: $2-$3

Plush Safari Babies (L to R): Hippo, Tiger, Alligator, Monkey, and Elephant.

Miscellaneous Plush

2000 to current
A wide variety of plush animals have been produced the last few years.

Value: $2-$3

A wide variety of plush dispensers have been produced for the European and American market.

Political Animals Elephant and Donkey

No Feet

This is an extremely rare dispenser, only a few are known to exist. It is thought to represent the elephant of the Republican political party. In early 1997 a file was discovered in the PEZ factory in Connecticut containing a press release and an old photo of a special set of dispensers. The press release was dated June 13, 1961, and had the heading "President Kennedy receives PEZ souvenirs on his visit to Vienna." It went on to detail the set and then said, "To the President of the United States of America J.F. Kennedy with the Compliments of PEZ." The set contained in a wooden, cigar like box had three dispensers; a Donkey for the President (to represent the Democratic Party), a Golden Glow for Jackie, a Bozo die-cut for Caroline, and three packs of candy for each. In 2006, the Donkey that was pictured in this set surfaced. It was found at the PEZ International headquarters in Linz, Austria. To date it is the only Donkey known to exist. The elephant pictured, is one of several known. This elephant example has a shiny golden colored head with his trunk extending over the top of his head.

Elephant:	**$6000+**
Donkey:	**$10,000+**

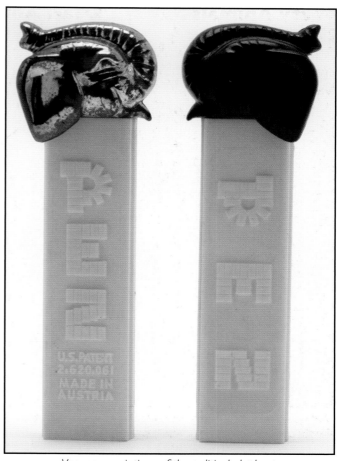

Very rare variations of the political elephant.

This is the only known example of this rare dispenser!

This rare dispenser is on display at the PEZ International headquarters in Linz, Austria.

A very rare political elephant with hard to find stand.

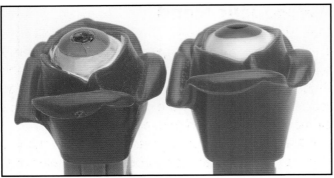

Close-ups of the vintage Psychedelic Flower (left) and the remake.

Psychedelic Flower

Late 1960s, No Feet

Very much a product of their time, these dispensers came packaged with flower flavor candy. They can be found with several different stickers including, "mod pez," "go-go pez," and different "luv pez" versions on at least one side. The side that has the sticker will be completely smooth. Some dispensers had stickers on both sides and are considered to be worth a bit more than a one-sticker dispenser.

A collector's edition remake was produced in the late 1990s and was available from PEZ through a mail-in offer. The remake versions have the raised PEZ logo on both sides of the stem and do not have stickers. They are also marked with a copyright symbol and 1967—the originals do not have a date on them.

Original: **$250-$350**

Remake, m.o.c.: **$5-$10**

Hard to find yellow and deep red flower variations.

Psychedelic Flower from the late 1960s.

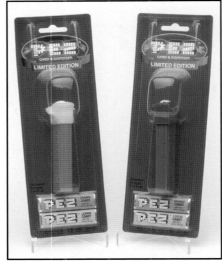

Collector's Edition Psychedelic Flower on card—these dispensers were available in 1999 through a mail-in offer.

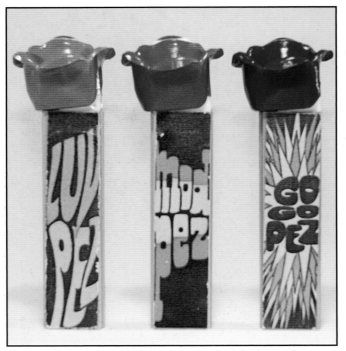

Three different color variations of the psychedelic flower dispenser.

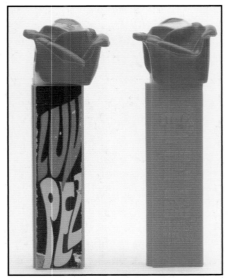

Comparison of a vintage Psychedelic Flower (left) and a Collector's Edition remake.

Psychedelic Hands from the late 1960s. The Black Hand on the right is a less common variation.

Psychedelic Hand

Late 1960s, No Feet

The Hand also came packaged with flower flavor candy, and will have at least one sticker. The side that has the sticker will be completely smooth. Some dispensers had stickers on both sides and are considered to be worth a bit more than a one-sticker dispenser.

A collector's edition remake was produced in the late 1990s and was only available through a PEZ mail-in offer. The remake versions have the raised PEZ logo on both sides of the stem and do not have stickers on either side. They are also marked with a copyright symbol and 1967—the originals do not have a date on them.

Original:	**$200-$250**
Original, Black hand:	**$250-$350**
Remake, m.o.c.:	**$3-$5**
Misfits Pink or Yellow:	**$30-$40**
Silver or Gold:	**$80-$100**

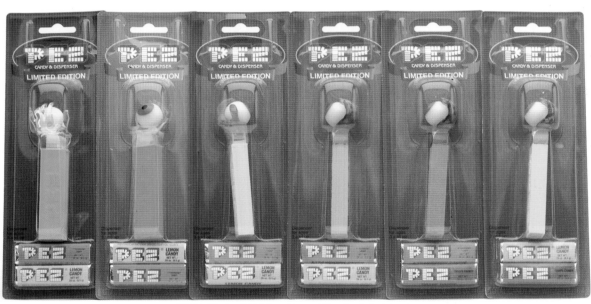

2001 Limited Edition Crystal Psychedelic Hands.

A collection of Black Psychedelic Hands.

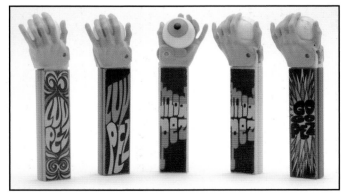

A collection Psychedelic Hands.

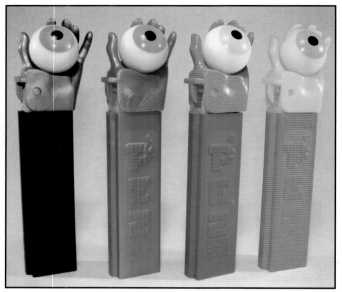

The silver and gold variations are hard to find, the pink variations were offered as part of the "misfits" line (mail-order offer).

Collector's Edition Hand on card—offered by PEZ in 1998 through a mail-in offer.

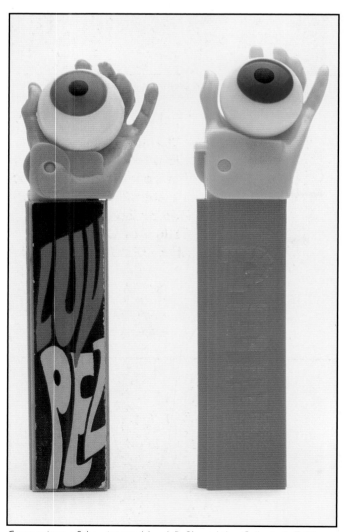

Comparison of the vintage Hand (left) and the Collector's Edition Remake.

Test pieces from the late 1990s.

Psychedelic Hand FX Toy Show

2005, No Feet

Five promotional dispensers could be purchased at the show for $5.95 each. There were also three different pad print color variations; one given to dealers/exhibitors, another to the first 500 people through the door and another to the people who purchased a three-day pass. A second set of dispensers was released in 2006, same premise; standard colors could be purchased at the show and a select few with special pad print colors were offered to dealers/exhibitors, first 500 through the door and two-day ticket holders. A special "decoder" dispenser was also offered.

Value: $10-$15

FX Toy Show held Jan. 27-29, 2006, in central Florida.

FX Toy Show premiums (2005).

FX Toy Show premiums (2006). Notice the decoder dispenser in the middle.

Robot (Also known as the Spacetrooper)

1950s

This is one of the few "full body" dispensers. They stand approximately 3-1/2" tall and have the letters "PEZ" on their back. Robots are tough to find.

Red or Blue:	$300-$350
Yellow or Dark Blue:	$325-$400
Shiny Gold (very rare):	$2500+

Advertising piece from the mid-1950s for the Ford Motor Company, this stand is extremely rare.

Robot or Spacetroopers from the late 1950s. A "full body" dispenser.

Back of blue robots.

Very rare gold robot.

Robots

These are actually the inside, candy-dispensing portion of the PEZ writing pen. Some collectors dismantle the pen to get to this dispenser. Some have been listed on eBay and other Internet auction sites as actual rare dispensers made by PEZ. While this statement is true, at least the part about it being made by PEZ, there is nothing rare about them. It's neat for display but always be aware and know what you are buying before spending big money.

Value:	**$1-$2**
Rocket Pen:	**$1-$2**

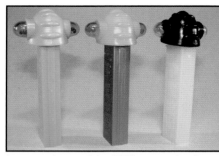

Inner workings of the PEZ pen make for a neat dispenser!

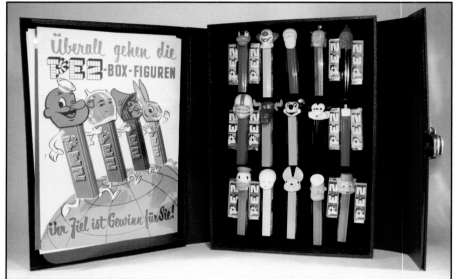

Salesman Sample Kit

Late 1950s early 1960s
This is a very rare sample kit that contains some classic dispensers and all the necessary paperwork.

Value: **$2000+**

WOW! A rare salesman sample kit from the late 1950s to early 1960s.

 Color crystal Sourz offered as a mail order premium.

Sourz

2002, With Feet
Released summer of 2002. Pineapple, blue raspberry, watermelon, and green apple come with new sour PEZ candy!

Value:	**$1-$2 each**
Crystal (clear or color):	**$5-$8 each**

 *Clear crystal Sourz offered as a mail order premium.*

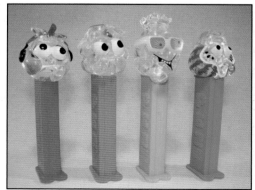

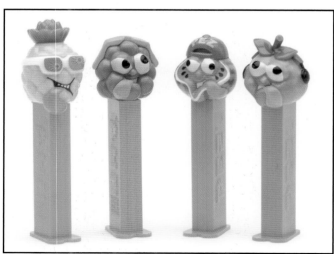

Pucker up! It's the Sourz dispensers!

Sparefroh

Early 1970s, No Feet

"Sparefroh" is German for "happy saver." October 31st of each year in Europe is World Savings Day when all people are encouraged to save money in a bank. (Thus the tie-in with the coin that is glued to the front of the stem.) This was a gift to children who put money in their bank account on that day. There are two different stem inscriptions: "110 Jahre Allgemeine Sparkasse in Linz" (this is the harder to find variation) and "Deine Sparkasse." The dispenser must have the coin attached to be considered complete.

Value: **$1200-$1500**

Sparefroh mint in the bag! Notice there is no candy in the bag, this dispenser came filled from the factory.

Sparefroh, a German dispenser from the early 1970s.

Stop Watch

2004

Interactive Sport Set contains a candy dispenser, real working stopwatch, whistle, and lanyard. European release.

Value: **$2-$3**

On your mark, get set, go PEZ! A real working stopwatch and dispenser.

USA Hearts

2002, No Feet

Mail-in offer. A set of six was offered for $8.95.

Value: **$5-$10 set**
Red crystal: **$2-$3 each**

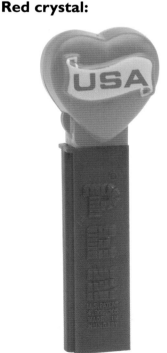

USA Heart.

Crystal version of the USA Heart (mail-order only).

Zielpunkt

1999, With Feet

Zielpunkt is a grocery chain in Austria. They commissioned PEZ International to immortalize their mascot "Smiley" in a unique and likable dispenser. This dispenser is not available in the U.S.

Value: **$15-$20**

Zielpunkt, a grocery store chain in Austria, commissioned PEZ International to produce a dispenser of their mascot "Smiley."

Ad sheets were only distributed to "people in the business"—salesmen, brokers, dealers, etc. They were not meant for the general public, making them difficult to find. Some collectors pursue only the dispensers and have little interest in these sheets. Others enjoy collecting anything related to PEZ.

You can learn a lot by studying ad sheets—such as how dispensers were packaged, who distributed them, how much they cost. Rare and unusual color variations of some dispensers have been verified using information and pictures provided on some vintage sheets. Depending on the dispenser(s) pictured, size of the ad, and art work, prices for these ad sheets can go from a couple of dollars for a current ad to a couple of hundred dollars for a vintage ad of a popular character(s) like the Universal Studios movie monsters.

Around 2005 PEZ stopped producing and distributing these sheets. Currently dealers can get an electronic version that provides much of the same information. Salesmen now use a printed booklet to share up-coming offerings with retailers or on special occasions, such as a candy industry show, the company will have a few paper copies to distribute to interested buyers. The days of cool, old paperwork distributed far and wide seems to be a thing of the past.

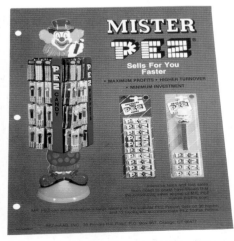
Superheroes ad sheet. $30-$40.

PEZ ad sheet from the 1960s. $50+.

German ad sheet from the 1970s. $25-$40.

Spinner rack ad sheet from the 1970s. $30+.

PEZ Pal ad sheet from the 1970s. $50+.

Pezi ad sheet from the 1960s. $50+.

Going back to its roots by promoting an adult breath mint, the remake of the PEZ regular from the 1990s. $2-$4.

Psychedelic ad sheet from 1967. A very desirable ad sheet. To date, no counter box as shown in the ad has been found. $350+.

Reverse of the psychedelic ad sheet.

Candy brochure from the 1990s showing the PEZ factory in Orange, Connecticut. $4-$8.

German ad sheet from the 1970s. Notice the Doctor does not have hair. $20-$40.

PEZ Pal ad sheet from the 1970s. Notice that the Engineer, Stewardess, Pilot, and Sheriff all appear to be prototypes and not actual production pieces. $20-$40.

Batman ad sheet from around 1965. $200+.

Muppets sales sheet from 1991. If you look closely you will notice the dispensers pictured are prototypes and not actual production pieces. In order to promote an upcoming line before it comes out, many times production pieces are not available in time to use with the advertising. $3-$5.

Back of the Batman ad sheet.

Universal Monster ad sheet from the 1960s. Front and back pictured. $400+.

Make-a-Face and Olympic Wolf advertisements from a Croatian magazine. This is the only ad for a Make-a-Face I have ever seen. $20-$35 each.

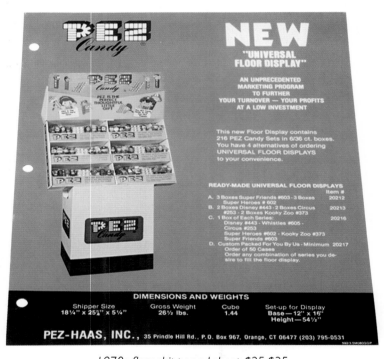

1970s floor shipper ad sheet. $25-$35.

Holiday advertisements with animated Santa and Snowman and an ad from 1979 with Disney characters. It seems a large variety of these ads were done from the early '70s to the early '80s in Croatia. They are printed on cheap paper similar to newspaper. Many different ads can be found in on-line auctions for a reasonable price. Most ads $10-$15 each.

Snow White ad sheet from the 1960s. $75+.

Counter display cards from the 1950s approximately 5"x7". $30-$40 ea.

Cool! Inside the costume book.

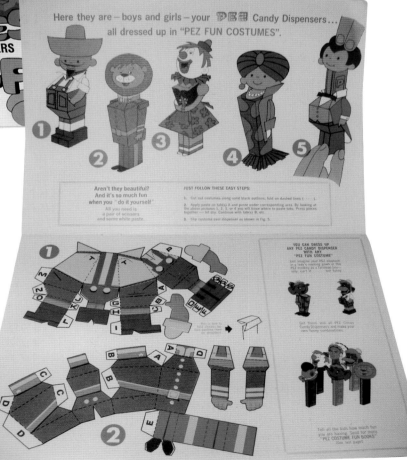

Mail-in premium from the 1970s. $150-$200.

This ad is from 1929 and is one of the oldest advertisements known for PEZ Candy.

Ghoul paper mask offered as a premium in the 1970s. $200+

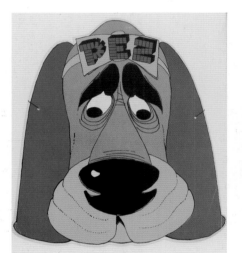

Dog mask paper mask offered as a premium in the 1970s. $100+

Hobo paper mask offered as a premium in the 1970s. $100+

Caveman paper mask offered as a premium in the 1970s. $100+

Pirate paper mask offered as a premium in the 1970s. $100+

Woman paper mask offered as a premium in the 1970s. $100+

This is the only known example of this board game from the 1920s. As you travel the path through the land of Haas, you will see advertisements for many of their products including four different PEZ illustrations. $2500+.

The first to finish was rewarded with a pile of Haas goodies!
(Notice the PEZ drops and Pez peppermint pack both pictured).

Center illustration on the board game shows the PEZ drops (notice the candy is round).

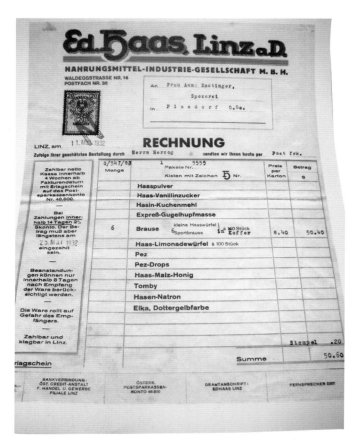

Vintage Haas receipt dated May 11, 1932. Both PEZ and PEZ drops are listed as choices on this invoice.

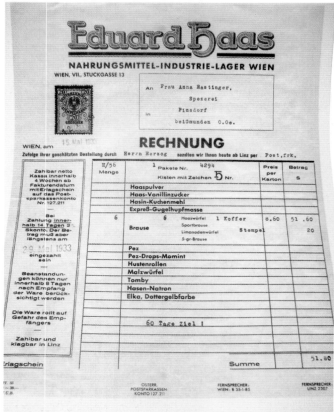

This invoice is dated May 15, 1933. Both PEZ and PEZ drops are listed as choices on this invoice.

Wow! PEZ International booth from the 1970s loaded with goodies!

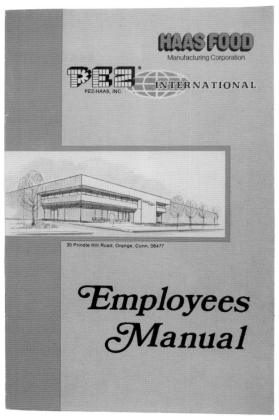

1970s/1980s employee manual.

Outdoor event promoting PEZ in the 1950s—cool tablet shaped tables!

Thirty fresh cases of PEZ from the 1970s.

1950s advertisement for the full body Space Trooper.

European PEZ Volkswagen delivery van from the early 1950s.

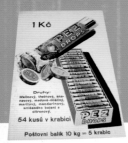

CHAPTER 19

While the candy itself has always been at the core of the business, collecting the individual candy packs has limited interest among PEZ collectors. The desire to find odd and unusual candy packs has piqued some collector's interest, causing prices to rise into the hundred-dollar plus range for some rare packs. Examples of rare candy packs include those that have pictures of a regular on the back, small sample packs from a tradeshow that only contained three or four pieces of candy, or simply a flavor that did not sell well such as flower flavor from the 1960s. These kinds of packs are very difficult to find and therefore command higher prices.

Condition, flavor, and language are the three most important factors when determining the value of a candy pack. Age also plays a part—generally the older the pack the higher the price. The ingredient list on the side also plays a part but should be considered more of a variation than a value factor.

In the late 1990s, candy packs were modified and manufactured with the label printed right on the foil. Currently, these have little value beyond retail price. Earlier packs that have a paper label separate from the foil will be more desirable as candy pack collecting gains interest. Prices for candy packs can vary as widely as the many variations that can be found.

Known PEZ flavors include: Anise, Apple, Assorted Fruit, Cherry, Chocolate, Chlorophyll, Coffee, Cola, Eucalyptus–Menthol, Flower Flavor, Grape, Hot Cinnamon, IZO (vitamins), Lemon, Licorice, Lime, Mint, Orange, Peppermint, Raspberry, Strawberry, Sour Blue Raspberry, Sour Pineapple, Sour Green Apple, and Sour Watermelon. Many of the less popular flavors, such as Flower and Chlorophyll, were quickly discontinued making the candy packs quite scarce.

Of the old candy packs that have survived, much of it has held up very well. The exception seems to be European candies from the late 1980s and into the '90s. Most every collector who has been at this a while will have the same story to relate, many packs from this era have softened and leaked onto the card leaving a stained, sticky mess behind. Climate plays a big factor in preservation, if you plan on collecting candy, keep them stored in a cool dark place that has a consistent temperature and low humidity. A good way to re-use those small desiccant packages (silica gel) found in the pockets of some clothing or packed with certain pieces of electronic equipment are to store them with your candy packs. They are great for absorbing excess moisture and help to preserve the candy. Most, if not all of these desiccant packages are marked "do not eat" but it's always best to keep them up and out of reach of any children.

Vintage Café candy pack from the 1960s. $200+.

Examples of various cherry-flavored candy packs. Some are rather tough to find such as the twin packs from the 1970s. $1-$20+.

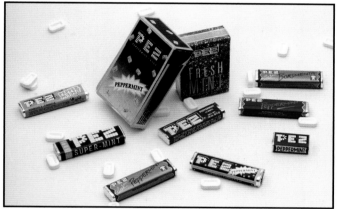

Peppermint refills. Some are hard to find such as the Super Mint and the small sample pack on the right. $1-$20+.

Strawberry refills. The "Erdbeer" (German for strawberry) and long pack in the back can be tough to find. $1-$15+.

Various candy packs. The two on the right offering a mail-in premium are tough to find. $1-$20+.

Grape refills. The Golden grape and the top center pack with the fruit pictured are tough to find. $1-$20+.

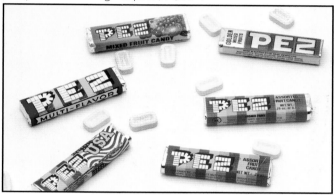

Various multi-flavor packs. The one marked "Pez USA" was not intended for U.S. sales, instead it was sold in eastern Europe in the late 1990s and advertised as a piece of "Americana." (Also notice the Kosher pack, middle right). $1-$15.

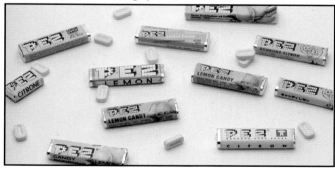

Lemon refills. The small sample pack on the left is hard to find. $1-$20+.

Orange refills. $1-$20+.

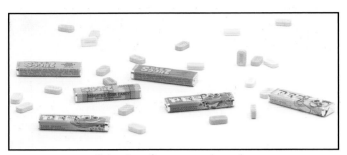

Selection of newer candy packs.

Various candy packs, the Eukalyptus Menthol pack is very difficult to find. $100+.

Box candy from Europe. $4-$8 each.

Various box candies from Europe. $5-$10.

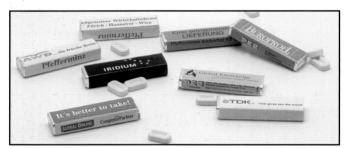

A variety of advertising candy packs. $3-$10 each.

Miscellaneous candy packs. (Clockwise from top) Choco: $30-$40; Lime: $50-$75; SIXO pack is quite rare: $75-$85; Red label Traubenzucker: $15-$20; Raspberry from Czech Republic: $.50-$1; TAB pack (and Austrian game manufacturer): $20-$30; Luftansa pack is from the German airline commemorating a Y2K party held in Munich on 12-31-99; McDonald's pack was found only in Austria, shown both front and back: $3-$5; 2000 Cola: $1-$2.

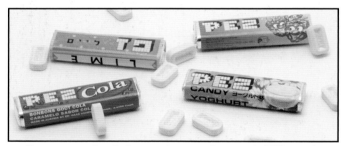

Some unusual variations and rare yoghurt pack. $50+ each.

Various multi-pack refills. Notice the original price tag (bottom left) of 34¢!

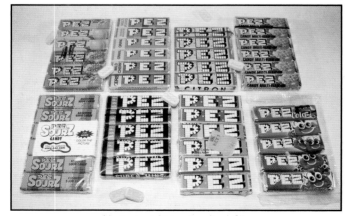

Various multi pack cello refills.

Various advertising candy packs. $2-$20.

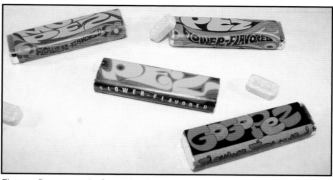

Flower flavor candy from the late 1960s these packs are extremely rare. $200+.

A selection of advertising candy packs. $2-$15.

Back view of the rare flower flavor candy packs.

Hard to find candy packs from the 1950s advertising the "Pez Box" dispenser on the back. $125-$175 each.

Grape refills. The Golden grape and the top center pack with the fruit pictured are tough to find. $1-$20+.

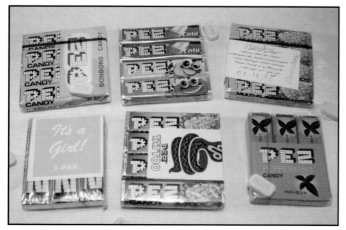

Various small cello pack refills.

A selection of Doppel (double) packs and some long packs. $20-$40.

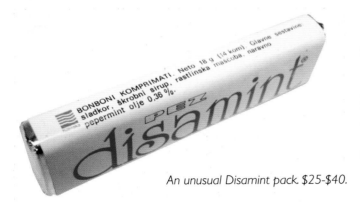

An unusual Disamint pack. $25-$40.

This is one of the oldest candy packs known to exist. From the mid 1930s when PEZ was transitioning from the round candy drops.

Vintage liquorice pack from the 1960s. $200+.

Back of the liquorice pack.

It appears the man pictured on the pack was a boxer or athlete and the perforations in the wrapper indicate the picture was probably meant to be separated and saved much like a trading card. Loosely translated the writing says:
"everyday a gymnastic (sport) lesson
every hour a gymnastic pez
this keeps you fresh and healthy"

Vintage tooling dies used to make the individual pieces of candy. Various die sizes used to make the candy have been discovered in the last few years. $150-$250 per pair.

Notice the candy is still round!

A selection of miscellaneous candy packs. The small blue sample packs are from a TGI Fridays restaurant in Russia. (NEU is PEZ in Russian). $3-$25.

A selection of mini candy packs: $1-$60 for some of the old vintage packs pictured in the bottom row.

Simpsons, Garfiled, Lord of the Rings, Mr. Bean, Spider-Man, and Franklin the Turtle are all part of a numbered series of candy packs, called "fun cards" that appeared briefly in Europe around 2002. Each pack had a different picture and number. There were 35 or more different packs in each series. $2-$3 ea.

A selection on long candy packs on the left $10-$25; Fruit gum $20-$30; Tomby caramel candy packs $25-$35; and a smoke-pause pack $15-$20 (still trying to offer an alternative to smoking in the 1960s).

A selection of hard to find twin packs. $40-$60.

An assortment of miscellaneous candy packs. The two "free sample" packs pictured in the middle are extremely rare. $200+. The "super mez-menta" pack is a vintage knock off of a PEZ candy pack.

Porcelain metal advertising sign. Probably from the mid to late 1950s.

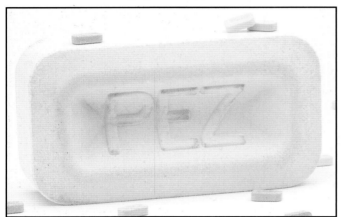

Giant piece of PEZ candy! These are created as a gift at certain European factories for potential customers or visiting VIP's.

Supermint European advertising poster-probably late 1950s early 1960s. $200+.

Candy sample pack from the 1950s. These were usually given away at candy conventions or trade shows. $150+.

Inside shot of sample pack.

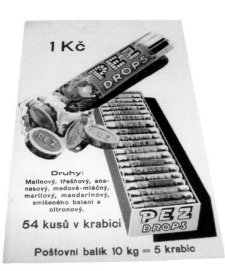

Late 1920s advertisement. This may be the oldest known ad showing the round PEZ drops.

Slightly larger than a matchbook, the outside appears to be an advertisement for "Austrobus."

Vintage ad introducing the new "color-rich" point of purchase display box.

Back of the sample pack.

Two free candy samples and a multi language PEZ advertisement touting the wonderful benefits of PEZ.

Front cover of a candy ad featuring the "Pez flavor girls" early 1960s.

Inside of ad announcing the new flavor.

Candy pack ad sheet from the 1950s.

Cool old wrapper from the Czech Republic!

PEZ Drops wrapper from the late 1920s!

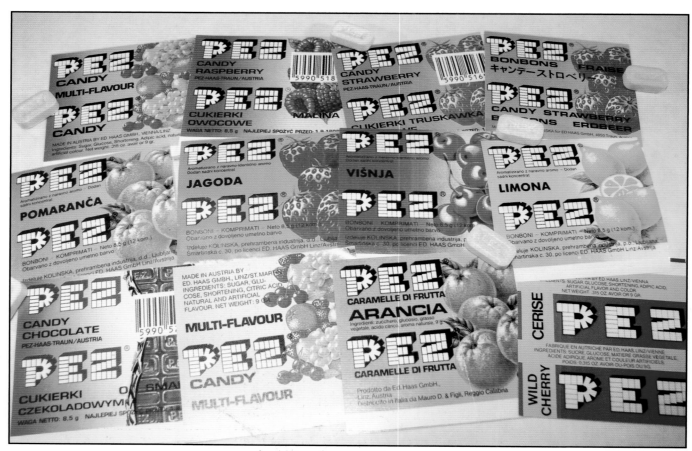

A selection of newer candy wrappers.

The American version of the new mini mints featuring works from Norman Rockwell. $1-$2 ea.

The European version of the new mini mints featuring works from Andy Worhol. $1-$2 ea.

European version of the new mini mints featuring vintage PEZ girl artwork. $2-$3 ea.

Fizzing vitamin candy tablets from Europe. $5-$10 each.

Vintage counter boxes can be expensive and tough to find. It was, and still is considered a disposable item. When the product was gone the shopkeeper threw the box away and ordered another—it was never meant to be saved. Most of the vintage boxes contained 24 or 36 dispensers, which means there was only one box for every two or three dozen dispensers. Consider the relatively small quantity that have survived compared to the number that was once produced. Made of plastic, the dispenser was meant to be played with, and likely ended up in a toy box or bottom of the junk drawer. The boxes on the other hand, made of cardboard and paper, were designed for the express purpose of merchandise display and discarded when empty. If, for example, a dispenser is valued at $100, in theory that should dictate the price of the box would be 24 to 36 times that of the dispenser—current prices are nowhere near that range. When you look at it this way, it's easy to see how scarce some of these boxes really are. Prices are high for most boxes from the 1960s and '70s, but have the potential to go much higher if interest in collecting grows. Pricing an old counter box depends on the condition, size, rarity, characters or theme depicted, and the artwork. Boxes, like ad sheets, inserts, and other paper related items are not popular with all collectors. Boxes that were produced for a specific group are much harder to find and usually bring more money than generic boxes. Most of these were produced in the early to mid 1960s and are called "single theme boxes" because they had one specific purpose. Single theme boxes include such characters as The Jungle Book, Popeye, Batman, and Green Hornet. Boxes showing a generic character allowed more flexibility in what was placed inside them and quickly became more common in the 1970s and beyond. Around 2005, the company switched from a generic 24-count box to a single theme 12-count box for bagged dispensers. Given that these newer boxes are theme specific and the merchandise is being sold for a much shorter time period, I feel there is good potential for the newer boxes to increase in value.

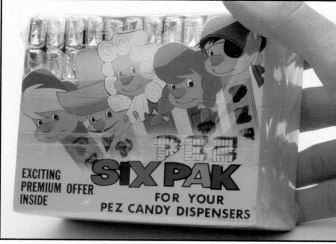

A rare "six pak" refill box from the 1970s. Notice the Admiral on the side: $400+.

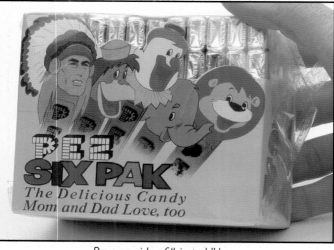

Reverse side of "six pak" box.

Single pack refill box from the 1970s. $400+.

Reverse side of single pack box.

Orange refill box from the 1980s. $25-$35.

Orange refills and box from the 1950s. Box: $100+; Candy packs: $20-$40.

1960s "brick" of Golden PEZ refills. $200+.

Cola candy box, and 8-pack refills. Refills: $6-$12.

Canadian fruit flavor refills with counter box.

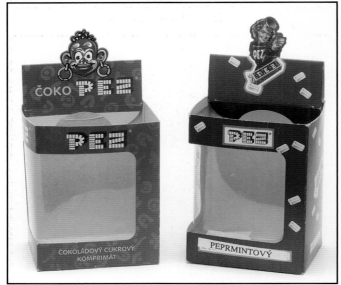

Candy refill boxes from Europe. Early 1990s. $5-$10 each.

1950s shipping carton that held two-dozen Peppermint refill boxes. Items like this are very tough to come by but have little interest for most collectors. $50+.

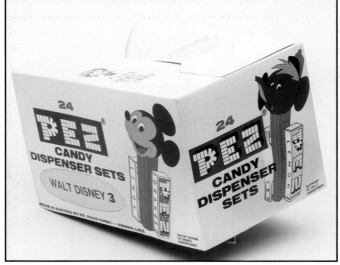

Outer cover of a 1970s counter box: $100+.

Disney counter box from the 1960s: $200+.

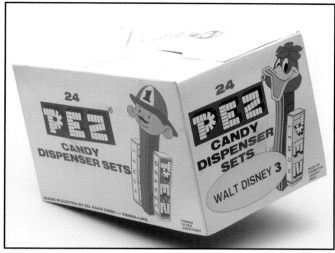

Reverse side of 1970s counter box.

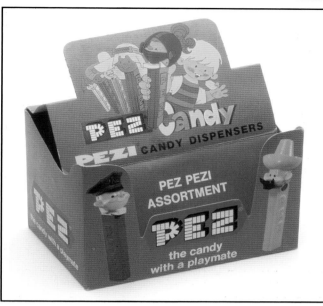

1970s PEZ Pal box: $150+.

Late 1970s Superheroes box: $200+.

1970s Circus PEZ box: $150+.

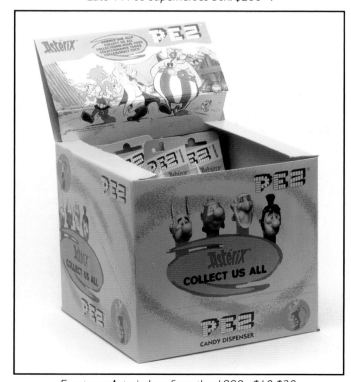

European Asterix box from the 1990s: $10-$20.

1970s Disney box: $200+.

Small single pack refill box with die-cut header. Dates to the 1950s. $450+.

Old cigar type box full of peppermint refills dating from the late 1940s. $2500+.

A rare Jungle Book box from the 1960s: $400+.

Japanese Peppermint refill box from the 1990s: $3-$5.

Japanese candy refill boxes from the 1990s: $3-$5 each.

Single pack refill boxes from the 1950s. These are very difficult to find and seldom turn up. $500-$750 each. (Notice the candy packs say "free sample"—these packs are extremely rare. $125-$175 each.)

Small acrylic box with blue embossed lid. This box dates to the 1950s. 250+.

Full boxes of Cherry and Traubenzucker candy packs. $200+.

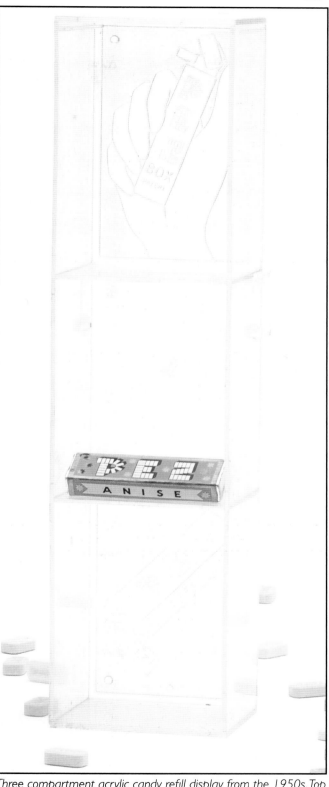

Three compartment acrylic candy refill display from the 1950s. Top compartment shows a hand dispensing candy from a BOX patent regular, the second shows how to set up the display and the third shows a single pack of peppermint candy. Display should have 2 small curved acrylic legs to be considered complete. The display box shows up occasionally but the legs are almost impossible to find. Display $200+; With legs $500+.

Traubenzucker display stand from the 1960s. $250+.

Rare die cut "flavor girl" refill box from the 1950s. $400+.

Rare "mini-toons" display box and mini-toons booklets. The booklets are described as "an action transfer product" and have a scene printed inside. Each booklet comes with a sheet of characters or objects that are designed to transfer to the booklet by rubbing over the picture with a pencil. Twenty-four different booklet titles from 1970. Box $500+; booklets $10-$20 ea.

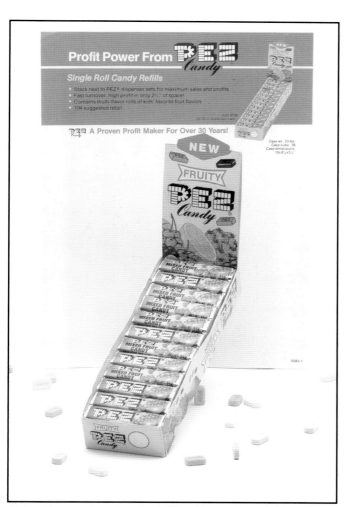

Fruit refill counter box from the 1970s with matching ad sheet. $250+.

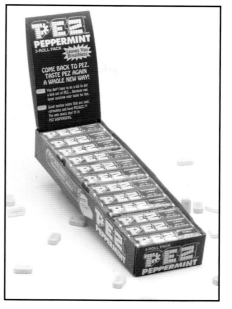

Peppermint refill counter box from the late 1990s. $10-$15.

Current candy refill display from Japan. $20-$30.

1970s counter display box. $100+.

Anise candy from the early 1950s, these boxes are extremely difficult to find. Notice there are two different variations pictured. $800+.

Display items
include wire racks, cardboard floor boxes, plastic tabletop
displays, and vending machines. Through the years, PEZ has relied little on advertising; instead they
choose to concentrate on eye-catching displays that prompt an impulse purchase.

Cardboard floor displays often feature various PEZ characters and attractive artwork that is themed
with the product for display. Some collectors may choose to only collect these cardboard header
signs as display racks can take up a lot of room but on the other hand the displays make great was
to show off your collection of packaged dispensers. Wire display racks typically found in grocery
stores often have cardboard header cards that have generic header on top.

In the late 1960s and through the 1970s, PEZ was also available in vending machines. The entry
of your local discount store often had a variety of vending machines geared toward attracting
the attention of a child. Everything from rubber balls, stickers, plastic rings, and candy were sold
in these machines, and PEZ was no different. Vending machines designed specifically for PEZ
were often part of the mix. The dispensers were packaged in small cardboard boxes and
usually contained a pack or two of candy. The boxes typically had the character's name or
picture printed on the side or maybe even a special offer advertising an
item only available by mail order. Vending boxes, once considered trash,
are now quite collectible and can be difficult to find.

1960s Bloomfield mfg. vending machine. A little over 4' tall, this thing weighs a ton! Great display piece, very desirable among collectors. In good to excellent condition: $2000+.

1990s cardboard floor shippers. Some stores will let you have the empty display making a great way to display or store your extra dispensers.

Peter PEZ spinner rack from the late 1980s early 1990s. $200-$250.

1970s cardboard Peter PEZ head for the top of a display rack. $85-$100.

Plastic Peter PEZ head. This was the top of a spinner rack display in the 1970s. $100-$150.

1970s cardboard floor display. $150-$200.

Ad sheet for vending machine. $75+.

Metal vending machine sign from the 1960s measures 12"x19." $350+.

Small 1970s wire rack. $150-$200.

Tabletop Peter PEZ display with acrylic bowls. From the 1990s, stands approximately 22" tall. $75-$100.

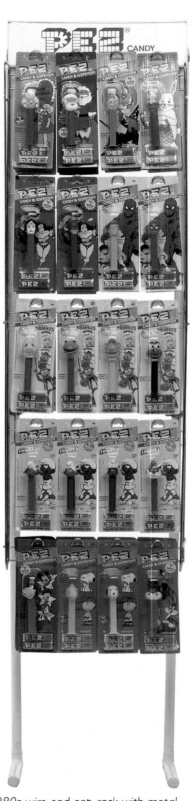

1980s wire end-cap rack with metal PEZ header sign. (Note: this was made to hang from existing store fixtures, the stand it is attached to is for photo purposes.) $100-$150.

Current wire display rack.

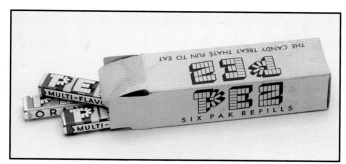

5-pack vending machine refill. $30-$40.

6-pack vending machine refill. $30-$40.

1970s vending machine boxes. (They will be worth more if the dispenser is still sealed inside the box.) $25-$35 each.

Unopened Mickey Mouse and Donald Duck vending machine boxes from the late 1960s/early 1970s. $50-$75 each.

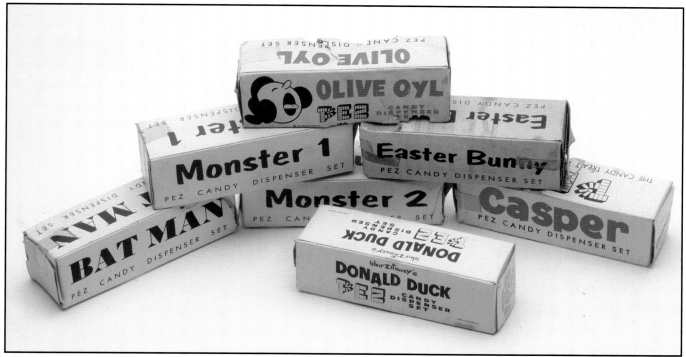

Various vending machine boxes from the 1960s (some boxes will be worth a little more depending on the character or art work). $40-$60.

PEZ Western header card from Europe. This is what PEZ sold in Europe in the mid-1970s in place of our Bicentennial series. Paperwork on this refers to the Indian Chief as "Winnetou," the Indian Squaw as "Winnetou's schwester" (his sister), and the Cowboy as "Old Shatterhand." $200+.

1950s cardboard window display. The ladies arm folds out to create a 3-D effect as if she were handing you a PEZ. A very rare item. $500+.

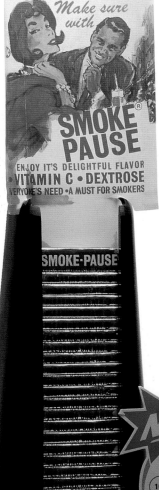

Smoke Pause display from the late 1950s made by Haas. It was sold as a breath mint for people between smokes. Individual candy packs: $15-$20. Display: $200+.

Metal candy pack refill carousel from the 1950s. This one is missing the loop and header card that attaches to the top of the display. Can also be found in a red and yellow alternating panel version. Without the loop and header: $200-$250. Complete: $350-$400.

Christmas, PEZ Pal and Kooky Zoo header cards from the 1970s. $75-$100.

Bicentennial, Circus, and Mr. Ugly header cards from the 1970s. $75-$100.

European coin tray made of a melamine-like material, measures approximately 7" square. It was placed on the counter near the cash register and used to return customers' change. $15-$25.

A very rare store display from the 1950s. She stands about 4 feet tall. $500+.

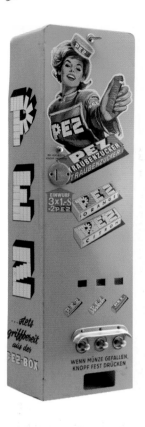

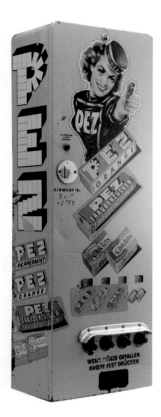

European wall mounted vending machine. Most of these are about 30 inches high and 10 inches wide, this particular model has been restored. Restored $250-$350.

European vending machine, these are gaining popularity among collectors. The trend seems to favor original machine over restored models. Original $300-$500.

New European spinner rack, four different versions exist, large circular, large semi-circular (for placement next to a wall), medium circular (three rows of hooks), and a medium semi circular. $150-$200.

This is one of the harder vending machines to find. The metal sign will turn up from time to time but a nice example of a complete machine is very difficult to find, 1960s. $2500+.

This vending machine dispensed "funny face" dispensers (a cheap imitation of PEZ) the same machine was also used to sell PEZ dispensers. Machines like this, especially examples in this nice of condition are extremely difficult to find, 1970s. $2000+.

Looks like a regular dispenser but this giant display stands just over six feet tall! Used in Europe for store display or promotional events, these displays are extremely difficult to find. Most that have made it to the U.S. have been damaged in some way during shipping. The display is non-functioning (i.e. the head does not tilt back) and has a weight in the feet to help keep it upright. $2000+.

A rare original example of a Pez lady outfit from the 1950s. $2000+.

The ladies in the photo are wearing the same uniform.

Peter PEZ "peg board" style display from the 1970s early '80s. $350+.

Double sided display rack that was exclusive to Toy 'R Us stores around 2003. The toy store stopped carrying carded dispensers and switched to poly bag display boxes that could be sold from existing store fixtures. Soon after the switch, stores were instructed to discard displays into the garbage. A lucky few collectors were able to salvage one of these great displays before they were destroyed. $250+.

CHAPTER 22

Miscellaneous

Advertising Items

PEZ has never relied heavily on advertising, so ad-related items are relatively scarce. More advertising items exist from Europe than from the U.S.

European theater programs from the 1940s and 1950s with PEZ advertisement. Notice the one on the left, they used candy pack stickers like this to seal the program. One side of the sticker was stuck to the front and the other to the back. You had to break the seal in order to look at your program. Also pictured candy tin sold from 1934-1950: $150+, and unusual French PEZ premium key chain: $30-$40.

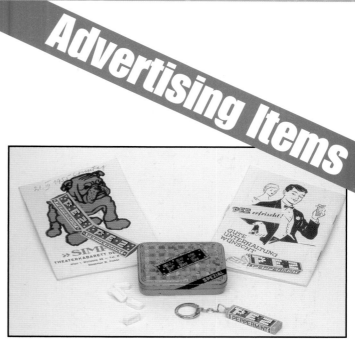

Comic ad from the 1980s and paper visors from the 1970s. Ad: $10-$15. Visors: $15-$20.

A rare European trolley or train advertising sign from the 1950s. Measures approximately 13"-17": $500+.

White Castle kids meal sack from 1990. The sack reads: "One Halloween Pez candy dispenser with every Castle Meal." $35-$45.

1970s PEZ paper sack from Europe. $25-$30.

Body Parts

Newer Body Parts (L to R): Indian, Soccer Player, Sheriff, Pirate, and Policeman. $10-$15 ea.

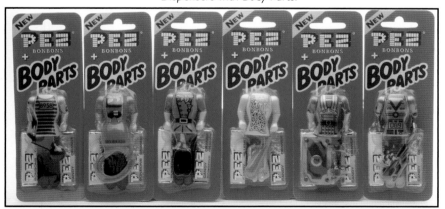

Dispensers with Body Parts.

PEZ introduced "Body Parts" in the mid-1990s. As the package states, "Body Parts are amusing attachable parts, with which you can dress up your PEZ dispensers." The pieces snap on around the stem of the dispenser. The arms are movable and the hands are designed to hold various items.

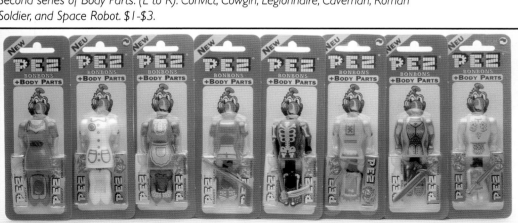

Second series of Body Parts. (L to R): Convict, Cowgirl, Legionnaire, Caveman, Roman Soldier, and Space Robot. $1-$3.

First series of Body Parts. (L to R): red dress, Nurse, purple dress, Hockey Player, Skeleton, Robin Hood, Knight, and Tarzan. $1-$3.

PEZ® Girls

An old photo showing the PEZ lady handing out candy samples at an outdoor event. This photo was taken in Europe sometime in the early 1950s.

Promotional "speaker box" had a sexy voice of a woman promoting the newest candy flavors. Not sold at retail this was sent to dealers and brokers as a way to encourage additional orders. 1960s $1000+.

Old photo of the "PEZ Girls."

Top of the box reads "let me tell you about the new 10¢ piece!"

In Europe the "PEZ Girl" was used on advertising into the early 1980's.

Tin European "postcards" with vintage artwork are from the 1990s and measure approximately 4"x6": $15-$20 each; European phone card holders from the 1990s: $2-$4 each; and PEZ phone card (bottom center): $30-$40.

Snow White and several Maharajahs on a pentagon base. The base is marked "Pez" and was a mail-in premium in the 1960s. Found in a couple of different colors, ivory, as shown, is the most common. It holds 6 dispensers. $125-$175.

Premium Offers and Inserts

PEZ has offered many premiums throughout the years and the premium insert sheets have become as collectible as the premiums themselves.

German premium offers from the 1970s. The backside has individual spaces to glue candy wrappers. When it got full you mailed it in and received the current premium in return. $5-$10.

1950s insert. $25-$35.

Reverse side of 1950s insert.

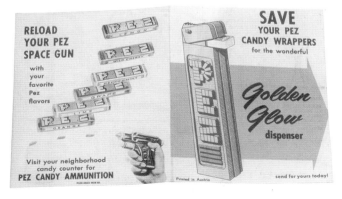

Rare 1950s space gun insert. The inside reads: "Dear Friend, COCOA MARSH is delighted to send you your free Pez space gun. Thank you for your continued loyalty to COCOA MARSH. We hope we can always live up to your families trust in us. With this in mind, we believe we have made COCOA MARSH with the finest chocolate syrup you can buy—the only leading chocolate syrup which contains vitamins B1, B2, D, and Iron. We hope, too, that you've had fun with our soda fountain pump. The best of health and happiness to you. Cordially, the Taylor-Reed Company, makers of COCOA MARSH." $65-$85.

Very hard to find comic ad from the 1970s featuring the rare Admiral. (Notice the pentagon stand offer is called "trophy pencil holder" and shows the Admiral dispenser in the back). $75+.

Bendie arms and legs; these were never sold at retail and are extremely rare. The salesman would slip them on a dispenser and leave it with a potential customer to help get the dispenser noticed. 1960s $500+.

Various inserts, the one on top is from the 1970s: $15-$20; bottom right is from the 1950s: $35-$40; and bottom left is from the 1980s: $4-$8.

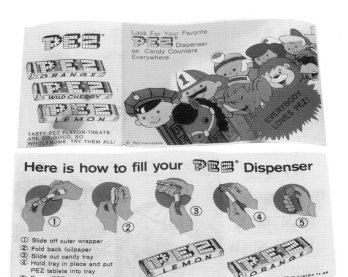

Front and back, how to load your dispenser insert. $10-$20.

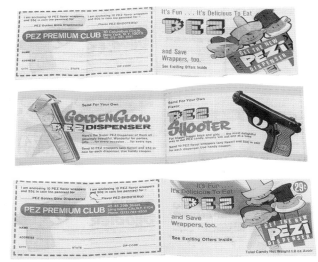

Front, back and variation of Pezi insert, from the 1960s. $20-$30.

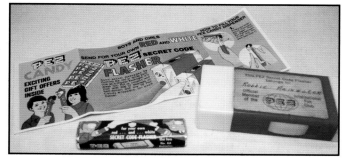

Golden Glow and candy shooter offers: $15-$25; inserts with characters: $25-$35.

Secret Code Flasher, Golden Glow, and T-shirt premium offer inserts. $15-$25.

Secret Code Flasher with insert and candy pack advertisement from the 1970's. Secret Code flasher: $250+; insert: $15-$25; candy pack: $25-$40.

Inside of European PEZ booklet. Measures approximately 4"x16." From the late 1950s or early 1960s: $40-$50.

Prototypes

Everybody's favorite hamburger guy, Ronald McDonald. This rare plaster prototype is one of only two known to exist. PEZ created it for McDonalds with the idea of making a Ronald McDonald PEZ dispenser for the Happy Meal. The idea was scrapped after it was realized the enormous quantity needed would completely shut down PEZ production to the point that they could make nothing but the one dispenser.

Prototypes are also known as mock-ups. They are often made of plaster or resin and are representations of dispenser heads before the dispenser is actually produced. Collectors may sometimes find prototypes for heads that were never produced.

Plaster mock-ups, very rare. (L to R): Three-piece Witch, Skull, Mr. Ugly, One Eye Monster, Octopus, and Creature.

Original tooling dies (L to R): Cocoa Marsh, Zorro, Hippo stem inscriptions, Duck Nephews, and Casper for the die-cuts, Football Player pennant, and a DBP 818 stem logo. The bottom die is a two-piece mold that made the candy buttons. $300+ ea.

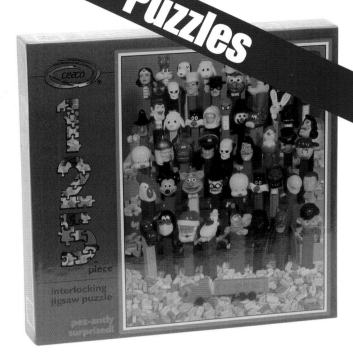

Puzzles

German frame tray puzzle from the 1970s. $25-$35.

Ceaco brand puzzle. This appeared for a very brief time in the early 1990s. It was pulled from market because the makers did not secure proper rights to use the licensed characters. 125-piece puzzle: $40-$50. There is also a 550-piece version: $50-$70.

Hallmark "Pezzazle" puzzle from the mid-1990s. $15-$20.

Stickers and Clickers

Stickers were included in many of the dispenser and refill packages in the 1970s.

Square sticker doubles from the 1970s. These were also free inside candy refill packages. $3-$6 each.

Round sticker doubles from the 1970s. These were free inside cellophane 6-pack candy refill packages. $5-$8 each.

Round sticker singles from the 1970s. These were a free premium offered inside some bagged dispensers. $5-$8 each.

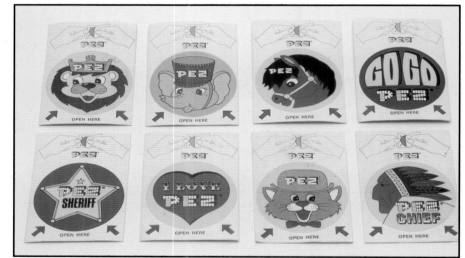

Various clickers. $15-$25 each.

Tattoos from the 1970s. $15-$25 set.

Clickers packaged like this are extremely rare. $200+.

1950s Boy and Girl "Pez Box" clicker $200+.

1950s peppermint candy pack clickers $10-$15 ea.

Unusual Packaging and Variations

Many packaging variations have been produced through the years. This is by no means a complete offering but a sample of some of the more unusual variations.

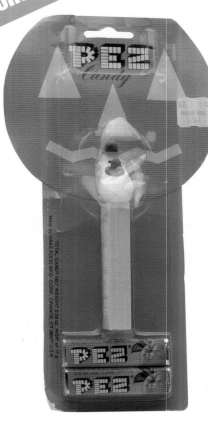

Clown with chin on a rare die-cut Halloween card. $200-$250.

The Captain with a Bicentennial header card. Header card alone: $40-$50.

Back side of the Fireman.

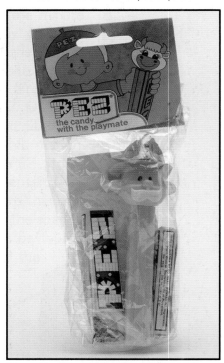

Fireman still in the bag (notice the white mustache, very unusual). $200-$250.

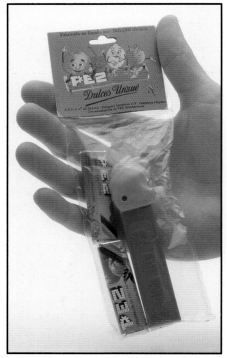

A Spanish-made dispenser mint in the bag. If you look closely you can see the country of origin on the stem is Spain. Dispensers marked Spain are very difficult to find. As pictured, $150-$200.

Donkey whistle still on original card. $100-$125.

Unusual Chinese packaging. $40-$50.

Unusual "PEZ Rallye" card. $200-$250.

Unique twin pack of glowing ghosts and a dinosaur gift pack, both only released in Europe. $10-$15 each.

2+12 Box sets (non-U.S.). The 2 meant you got 2 dispensers and the 12 meant 12 packs of candy. $5-$10.

Gyro Gearloose on Japanese bubblepack. The one on the left is the older version and the one on the right is the new updated version.

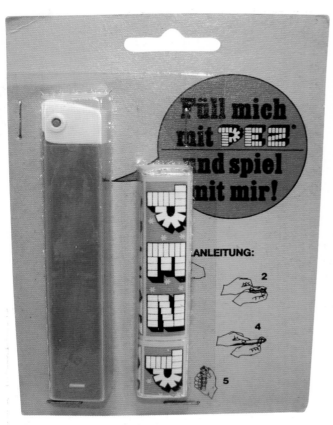

Regular on the card—notice the odd pack and a half wrapper on the candy. $150-$200.

Back side of the regular on the card.

Panda on small, square card $200-$250.

Back side of the Panda on card.

Odds and Ends

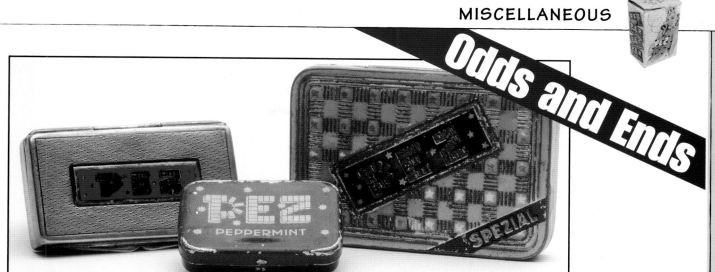

Original PEZ tins. Before there was such thing as a PEZ dispenser the candy was sold in tins like this. Very tough to find. The one on the left is from the early 1930s: $200+. The small blue one in the middle dates to 1927: $200+. The one on the far right was sold from 1934 to 1950: $150-$200. There is one other small round tin known with a picture of a car on top. It was called the "autobox": $500+.

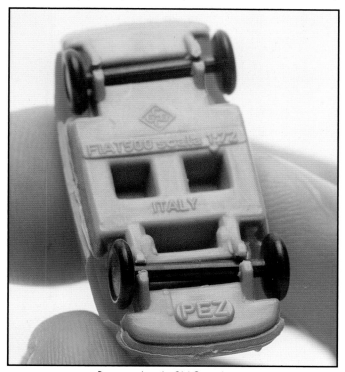

Bottom detail of H.O. scale car.

A very rare PEZ item, less than five are known to exist. Called a "magic viewer," by holding it up to the light and looking through the back, you could see color pictures of Canada's championship hockey team. Pull the lever on the side and another picture would rotate through. The last slide shows a black and white picture of the PEZ girl outside with skyscrapers in the background holding a regular. From the 1950s. $1000+.

H.O. scale cars. $3-$5 each.

Lapel pins from the 1960s. $5-$10 each.

Company envelopes and shipping label. $3-$5 each.

Various paper flags. $10-$15 each.

This is an ink blotter from France. It was common for companies to print their advertisement on these and give them away. This one dates to the 1950s and is tough to find. It measures approximately 4"-6." $25-$50.

Candy tin from the Czech Republic. Measuring approximately 10" long, 7" wide, and 4" tall, it held 8 boxes of single pack refills. It is from the mid to late 1990s these tins are hard to find. $75-$100.

Original candy tins from the late 1930s to 1950—notice the slight size difference in the two tins. The one on the left is slightly smaller than the one on the right. $150-$200.

European candy refill tin from the late 1990s early 2000. $50-$75.

European candy refill tin from the late 1990s early 2000. $50-$75.

European candy refill tin with an Egyptian theme from the late 1990s early 2000. $75-$100.

European candy refill tin featuring the PEZ lady from the late 1990s early 2000. $75-$100.

European candy refill tin featuring the Pez lady from the late 1990s early 2000. $75-$100.

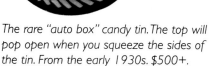

The rare "auto box" candy tin. The top will pop open when you squeeze the sides of the tin. From the early 1930s. $500+.

Counter display box for the PEZ pipes. $150-$200.

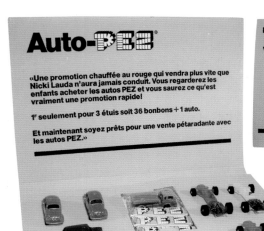

A rare example of a salesman's car display kit. 1970s $500+.

European pencil box premium from the mid 2000s $15-$20.

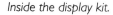

Inside the display kit.

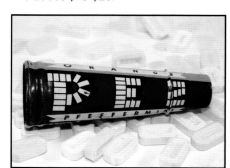

Rare, metal siren whistle from the 1960s. It's estimated there are about six of these known to exist. $300+.

New pull and go cars, the wheels are spring loaded so when you pull the car backwards and let go it will take of across the floor—and they dispense candy! Indy cars come in blue, red, and yellow. NASCAR style can be found in the same seven drivers as the helmet dispensers. $3-$5 ea.

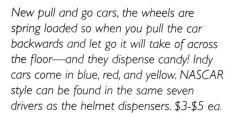

Front of Body's ad sheet.

Ingredients panel of the Body's dispensers.

Back of Body's ad sheet.

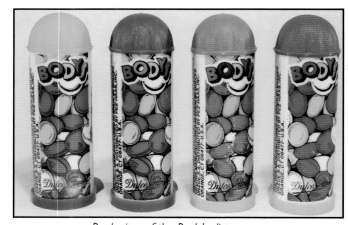

"Colorful, collectible space creatures filled with assorted fruit flavored space candies. Put them on display and watch them rocket right off your counter!" From the Body's ad sheet, six different characters were available in the 1980s. Very difficult to find $100+ ea.

School Tool candy dispenser features; PEZ dispenser, pencil, eraser, ruler, back pack clip, note pad, metric temperature converter, and metric distance converter! $1-$3 ea.

Back view of the Body's dispensers.

Hard to find metal yo-yo premium from the 1960s. $250+.

Unusual, rare item is believed to be a PEZ bank that was once offered as a premium. $500+.

Back view of the yo-yo.

Bootlegs

It is hard to determine the exact age of these dispensers, but it is apparent that they are old. There are no markings of any kind that can be found to give a hint as to the brand, manufacturer, or country of origin. What is also apparent in this group is they were clearly trying to borrow from the PEZ design. The dispensers are a thick, clumsy, poorly engineered version of a real PEZ dispenser. As seen in the photo showing the detail of the stem bottoms you can see how loose fitting the sleeve is inside the stem. The pig has an embossed stem with the letters "DAR"—it's anyone's best guess as to what these letters mean. DAR is a Spanish verb that means "to give," perhaps these were manufactured for the Spanish consumer? I would love to hear from anyone that has something different than what is pictured here or more information about these.

Comparison of a real dispenser on the left and bootleg on right.

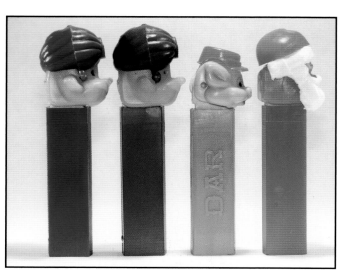

Profile shot of two Maharajas, DAR pig, and Santa.

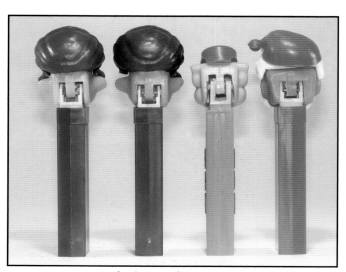

Back view of the group.

Do you want to meet other collectors? Have lots of fun? See more PEZ than you ever imagined? Attend a PEZ convention! Conventions are one of the best ways to get information and gain knowledge of the hobby, as well as to buy and sell PEZ. You will find many rare and unusual items displayed, as well as organized events such as "PEZ Bingo" to keep you busy.

Conventions have been sprouting up since the early 1990s, drawing people from all over the U.S and the world. Below you will find a current list of conventions, check **PEZ Collectors News** for exact times and dates.

Southern California – Conventions have been held since 1994 in several different locations with different hosts. Usually meets sometime in the spring.

St. Louis, Missouri – First convention held in 1993 and still going strong with the original host! Meets in June. Your host is John "Cool Pez Man" Devlin, who may be reached using the Web site, http://www.pezconvention.com or the 24-hour hotline: (314) 293-0179. COOLPEZMAN LLC 5541 Oakville Center #119 St. Louis, MO. 63129

Bloomington, Minnesota – First convention held in October 1996 across from the Mall of America. Now meets in August rather than October. Your hosts are Dana and Julie Kraft, they may be reached using the Web site, www.mnpezcon.com or write to: MN PEZ CON 7207 39th Street North, Oakdale, MN. 55128

Cleveland, Ohio – First ever PEZ convention, "Dispensor-O-Rama" held June, 1991 in Mentor, Ohio. Continues to meet each July in the Cleveland area. Your hosts are John and Linda Gliha. They may be reached using the Web site, www.pezamania.com or glidog@aol.com Write to them at: 1065 Conklin Road Conklin, NY. 13748 (607) 775-4793 after 5pm and before 10pm EST.

Connecticut – Called the "North East PEZ Convention" first met in April 1999 in Orange, Connecticut (home of PEZ Candy, Inc.). Moved to a larger location in Stamford, CT for the May 2000 show. Your host is Richie Belyski (editor of **PEZ Collectors News**) he may be reached using the Web site, www.pezcollectorsnews.com or at the following address:

PEZ Collector's News
P.O. Box 14956
Surfside Beach, SC 29587

In addition to the five major U.S. conventions Silvia Biermayr hosts the **Linz Gathering** in Austria. Conventions are usually held late summer. You may visit her Web site- www.pezing.com to get details or contact; Silvia Biermayr Posfach 74 A4070 Eferding Austria

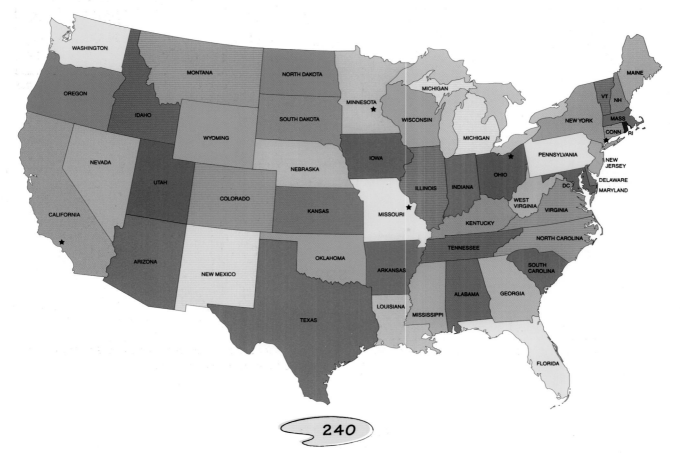

Convention Pins

The first California convention held in 1995, hosted by Steve Glew. "CA. CDC – California Candy Dispenser Convention" $10-$15 ea. Los Angeles Pez-a-Thon 2000 $15-20 ea.

Pezcific Coast Conventions pins from 2002-2007. $15-$25 ea.

Northeast Collectors Gathering pins 1999-2004. $15-$25 ea.

Northeast Collectors Gathering pins 2005-2007. $15-$25 ea.

2004 (top) and 2005 commemorative pin sets, proceeds from the sale of these sets were donated to charity. $30-$50 ea.

Thank you pin for those who donated items to the charity auction (same pin, different card). $25-$35 ea.

St. Louis convention pins (A.N.P.C.-Annual National PEZ convention). $15-$25 ea.

St. Louis PEZ convention pins 2005-2006. $15-$25 ea.

St. Louis pins from 2007. $15-$25 ea.

1998 St. Louis convention pin variations (printing on the stem is different). $15-$25 ea.

St. Louis pins from 2007, a pink and brown pin were also offered. $15-$25 ea. pink or brown $25-$40 ea.

Charity pin from 2006 St. Louis convention. $25-$40 ea.

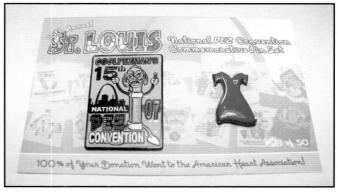

Charity pin from 2007 St. Louis convention. $25-$40 ea.

Cleveland convention pins 1995-1999. Notice the two variations (top row center) the pin on the right has an error—it's marked 1966 instead of 1996: $15-$25ea. Error pin: $25-$40 ea.

Cleveland convention pins 2000-2003. $15-$25 ea.

Cleveland convention pins for the 1st annual wars tournament. $25-$40 ea.

Cleveland convention pins 2004-2006. $15-$25 ea.

Cleveland convention pin 2007. $15-$25 ea.

Cleveland convention 2007 charity pin. $25-$40 ea.

Minnesota Pez Con buttons from 1996-1997. $35-$50 ea.

Minnesota Pez Con pins 2003-2005. $15-$25 ea.

Minnesota Pez Con pins from 1999-2002. $15-$25 ea.

Minnesota Pez Con charity pin set 2006. $25-$40 ea.

Minnesota Pez Con Dealer pin from 2006. $25-$40 ea.

Minnesota Pez Con pin from 2006. $15-$25 ea.

Erie Spectre pin set. $50-$75.

Back view of Erie Spectres pin set.

Linz gathering pin from 2007. $15-$25 ea.

Linz gathering pins from 2003-2006. $15-$25 ea.

*Pez-A-Go!Go! buttons and pin from the
Japanese conventions. $15-$25 ea.*

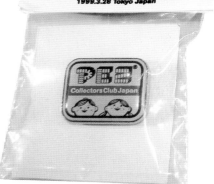

Pez-A-Go!Go! pins from 1998, 1999, 2000. $25-$40 ea.

This button says it all. $3-$5 ea.

Pezalicious pin. $10-$15 ea.

All of the pins pictured were created by collectors. None of these were issued by PEZ. $10-$20 ea.

Pez Con Alberta Canada 2002: $25-$40; Pez in the Sun: $15-$25; PCN pin: $15-$25 ea.

Pez Head list membership pin from 2007. $15-$25 ea.

PEZ Community pin. $10-$20 ea.

Several newsletters have been dedicated to collecting PEZ. The first, **The Toy Candy Container and Food Premium Collector**, appeared in 1987. With the third issue the name changed to **The Old Variety Store**. The **OVS** lasted until late 1989 and had a run of about 15 issues. In January 1990, the **Optimistic Pezzimist** came on board. It too had a run of just 15 issues, lasting until July of 1992. Without much delay, in the fall of 1992 the **Positively Pez** newsletter was started.

By this time the hobby was gaining steam. The first book about PEZ had been released during the previous year, and collectors were becoming more knowledgeable than ever. **Positively Pez** had a run of 19 issues and ended with the January/February 1996 edition. With the announcement of its close, and with an ever-growing number of collectors hungry for the latest PEZ information, two new publications were started. The **Fliptop Pezervation Society** premiered with the September/October 1995 issue, billing itself as "the first national club for PEZ collectors." Pedro PEZ, a boy PEZ Pal dispenser, was adopted as the club mascot and was sent around the world with various collectors visiting interesting places and having his picture taken.

Right on the heels of the **Fliptop** newsletter, **PEZ Collectors News** made its first appearance with the October/November 1995 issue. The two newsletters worked well together, uniting collectors and giving them more information than ever before. In December 1999, the **Fliptop Pezervation Society** announced that the September/October 1999 issue was their last and they would combine efforts with **PEZ Collectors News**. FPS enjoyed a run of 24 issues. Currently **PEZ Collectors News**, put out bimonthly by Richie Belyski, is the only newsletter devoted to PEZ. You can contact them at:

PEZ Collector's News
P.O. Box 14956
Surfside Beach, SC 29587
E-mail: info@pezcollectorsnews.com
http://www.pezcollectorsnews.com

PEZ IN SPACE

PEZ in Space? Cyberspace, that is. A ton of information about PEZ can be found on the Internet. It is an excellent source for up-to-date information and a great way to buy and sell PEZ. There are hundreds, maybe even thousands, of sites built by collectors that detail everything from how to properly load your dispenser to pictures of personal collections. A quick Google search of the word 'PEZ' will get almost 10 million search results!

One of the nicest collector-built sites is www. collectingpez.com . Good design, pictures, up-to-date information, and links to other Web pages make it a great place to visit.

Another great online source to gather information, meet other collectors and find out what's happening in the PEZ collecting world is the PEZHEAD list. Membership is free but you will need to register to read messages and post comments. Now, just over 1,300 members and growing, this is a quick up to the minute resource for collectors. Find it by going to www.groups.yahoo.com/groups/pezheads PEZ Candy, Inc. also has a Web site. Within their site you will find a FAQ list (Frequently Asked Questions), a list of PEZ Dispensers offered to date in the United States, a list of other cool PEZ products, information about PEZ newsletters, and the PEZ Store. The store sells many current dispensers and candy flavors, including some items that are unique and only available through the special mail-order program. The site can be found at: www.pez.com. Or you can visit the international PEZ web site- www.lets-pez.com

STARTING UP

If you are a new collector you are probably wondering how to get started. Start out slowly—look for all of the current release dispensers you can find around your town. That alone will give you a nice size collection on which to build without spending too much money. Most collectors ask the question: "Should I leave it in the package or open it up?" "Will it lose its value if I open it?" Opening the dispenser is a matter of preference. If the dispenser is old, I would advise against opening the package. With the new stuff, it's up to you. Personally, I buy at least three of each new release; one in the bag, one on the card to save, and one to open for display. It's true, a carded or bagged dispenser is traditionally worth more than one that is loose, but a dispenser out of package is more fun to display.

Next, move on to the current European dispensers. Most of these can be had for $3 to $4 each. Acquire all of these and the size of your collection will almost double. When it comes to vintage dispensers, decide what your first "price plateau" will be and start from there. For example, there are still a good number of footless dispensers that can be found for $25 or less. Once you buy all of these, move on to the next price level and so on.

Although some of the old dispensers reach into the hundreds and even thousands of dollars for a single dispenser, you don't have to spend your life savings to enjoy the hobby. Some collectors specialize and focus on collecting one favorite area such as the Animals or PEZ Pal series. Others focus on stems by collecting a character that is made in several different countries, or by collecting as many different colors as they can. A good example of this is the Teenage Mutant Ninja Turtles. There are eight different dispensers that come on eight different stem colors; if you were to collect all of the combinations you would have 64 turtles alone in your collection!

The most important thing to remember about collecting PEZ... collect what you enjoy and enjoy what you collect but most importantly.....it's a hobby— have fun!

BUTTON - A rectangle piece inside the stem, usually red but sometimes white, that the candy actually sits on. There are a couple versions: a rectangle with square corners, and a rectangle with rounded corners. The square corner version is the oldest.

CHANNEL - The groove on the front of the dispenser that runs the length of the stem.

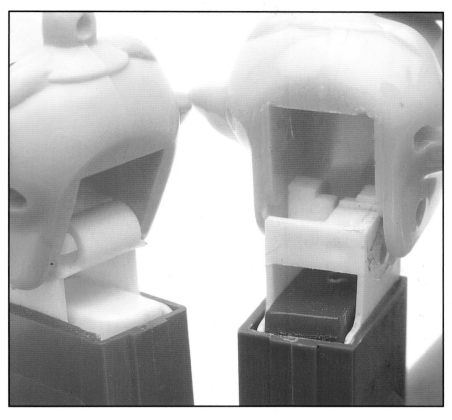

CLUB MED - A term used when a character's face appears very tan, as if they have been in the sun or at Club Med. This can also be considered a color variation.

COLOR VARIATION - Refers to the comparison of like dispensers in which one has a different color to the entire head or to one or more of the parts found on the head. Example: a cow may have a head that is yellow, blue, orange, green, etc. The possibilities are almost infinite.

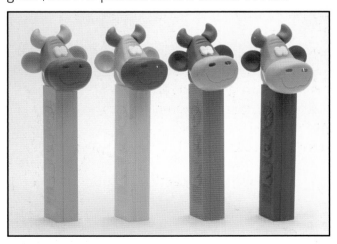

COUNTRY OF ORIGIN-

refers to the country in which the dispenser was made.
USA, DBP, Spain, Mexico, Brazil, Yugoslavia stems with half flowers are all highly desirable among collectors.

DBP - The German patent number on a dispenser. It means "Deutsches Bundes Patent" and will be accompanied by the numbers 818 829.

FEET - Small rounded plastic protrusions or tabs at the base of the stem to help the dispenser stand upright. Feet were added to dispensers in the U.S. around 1987. Currently there are 2 different styles. The earlier version is known as "thin feet," referring to the fact that the plastic of the feet is not as thick as the plastic feet found on current dispensers. Beware, some people try to cut the feet off and pass them off as a footless dispenser. Some dispensers were produced both ways, with feet and without. Look to the spine of the stem as a way to tell if it has been altered.

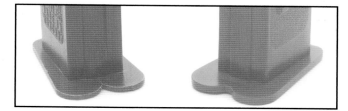

HEAD - The top-most part of the dispenser that tilts back to dispense the candy.

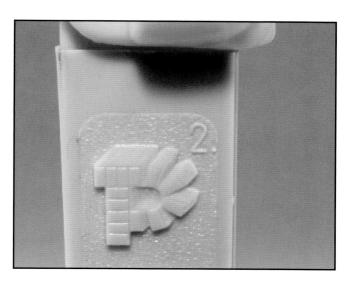

IMC - Injection Mold Code. A single digit number found on the outside top corner of the stem. Identifies in which plastic factory the dispenser was molded. Not all dispensers have IMC's. Here is a list to help identify which number goes with which country:

1 & 3 - Austria/ Hungary
2 - Austria/ Hong Kong
4 & 8 - Austria
5 - Yugoslavia/ Slovenia
6 - Hong Kong/ China
7 - **Hong Kong/ Austria/ Czech Republic**
9 - U.S.A.
V - **Yugoslavia (changed to Slovenia in 1993)**

KICKER - Sometimes referred to as the "pusher," this is the small plastic piece that extends down from the back of the head and pushes out a single piece of candy when the head is tilted back.

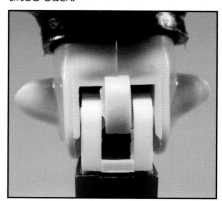

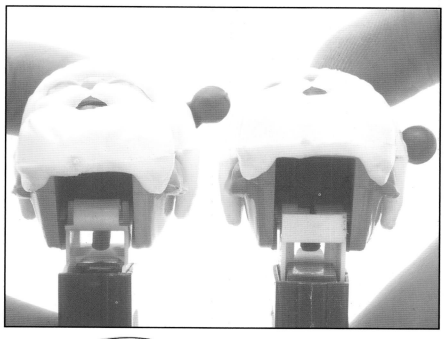

LOOSE - the dispenser is out of its original packaging.

MARBLEIZED - a term used when two or more colors of plastic are combined and not thoroughly mixed, causing a swirling pattern to appear in the finished product. This is a sought after variation by some collectors.

MELT MARK - refers to damage on the dispenser. Sometimes caused by direct heat or a chemical reaction between the plastic of the dispenser and certain types of rubber or other plastics. Certain types of rubber bands and items like rubber-fishing worms have been known to cause melt marks when left in contact with a dispenser.

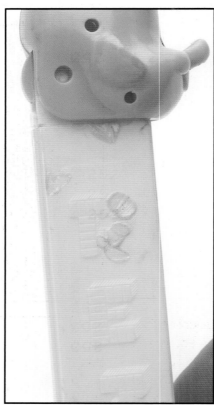

M.I.B. - Mint In Bag. Bag will have colored ends and writing as well as the PEZ logo. Newer style. Also known as a "poly bag."

M.I.C. - Mint In Cellophane or Mint In Cello. Bag will be clear with no writing.

M.O.C. - Mint On Card.

M.O.M.C. - Mint On Mint Card. Both dispenser and card are in pristine condition.

N/F - No Feet.

PATENT NUMBER - Seven digit number located on the side of the stem. Currently there are six different U.S. patent numbers on PEZ dispensers: 2,620,061 is the earliest, followed by 3,410,455; 3,845,882; 3,942,683; 4,966,305; and 5,984,285. 3,370,746 was issued for the candy shooter and appears on the 1980s space gun as well. Patent numbers can help identify the age of a dispenser but generally do not play a part in its value. Not all dispensers have a patent number on them, certain dispensers have no patent numbers, and this does not affect the value of those dispensers. Feet first started to appear on dispenser bases when the 3,942,683 number was issued but some exceptions can be found with feet and earlier issue patent numbers. These dispensers are difficult to find and carry a little more value with some collectors. Rare Italian made dispensers carry the patent number BREV. ITAL No.461637 Mexico dispensers have the mark 'Mexico Patent NR 141 242 both are extremely difficult to find.

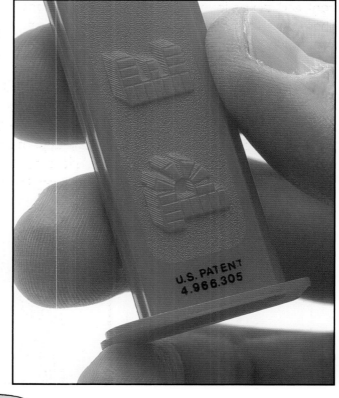

PEZHEAD - A term used to describe someone who collects PEZ!

PIN - Steel pin that hinges the head. Made of metal and found only in older dispensers. The pin runs through the side of the head and the sleeve, attaching it to the dispenser base.

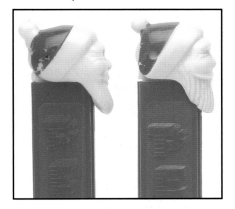

SHOES - An accessory for your dispenser that fits on the base of the stem. Similar to feet in that its purpose is to give the dispenser more stability when standing upright. Originally made to be used with the Make-a-Face dispenser. Reproduction shoes have been made with a rounded toe in the front, and can be found in multiple color variations. There is also a reproduction glow-in-the-dark version. An original shoe will always be black and have a "B" shape to the end.

SLEEVE - The part of the dispenser that pulls out of the stem and holds the candy. The United States patent description refers to this part as the magazine.

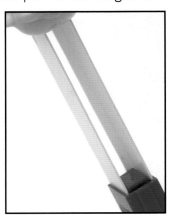

REGULAR - The earliest PEZ dispensers. These didn't have a character head; instead they had only a thumb grip at the top and were marketed for adults. These were remade in the late 1990s but with a noticeable difference. Vintage regulars will have a raised thumb grip on the top of the cap. The remakes will have a square cap with no raised grip and the spine will be deeper than the channel.

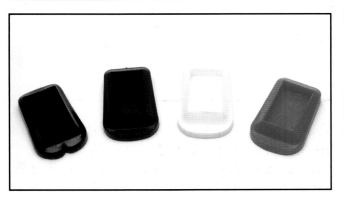

SOFTHEAD - The head is made of a rubber, eraser-like material that is pliable and softer than traditional plastic head dispensers, hence the name "softhead." Softheads can be found in the Erie Specter and Superhero series, along with a very rare Disney set that never made it to mass production.

SPINE - The groove on the back of the dispenser that runs the length of the stem. On a vintage footless dispenser the spine should be the same depth as the channel. Some unscrupulous people will try to pass off a dispenser as footless by cutting off the feet and claiming that it is old. To detect tampering, turn the dispenser upside down and compare the spine to the channel. The spine on a footed dispenser will usually be deeper than its channel.

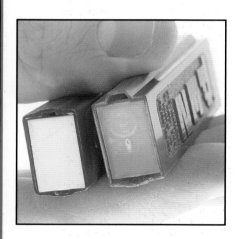

TRANSITION PIECE - A dispenser that has characteristics of a previous model but also has features of a current dispenser. These pieces must still be in their original packaging to show they are void of alterations. Example: an old style character head that is on a footed stem.

W/F - With Feet.

SPRING - Refers to either the spring inside the stem directly under the button, OR the spring in the top of the dispenser that keeps tension on the character head. There are 3 basic types of springs in the top of the dispenser: the classic wire mechanism, the blade spring, and currently a "leaf spring" mechanism.

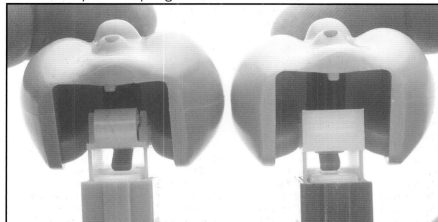

STEM - The lower part of the dispenser. Usually has the PEZ logo on at least one side and possibly country of origin, patent number, and injection mold code. Depending on the dispenser, the stem may also be die-cut or be completely smooth on one or both sides.

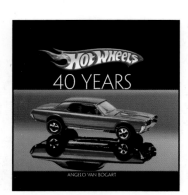

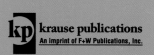
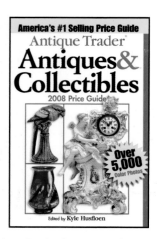
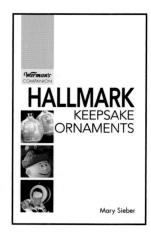